A HIGH and HOLY CALLING

D1225697

When Christ's people, the baptized,
gather for worship
they receive God's love
in word and sacrament,
and through the gift of music,
pray, praise, proclaim & recount
the story of God's grace in song.

The cantor...
the historical term
among Lutherans,
is the leader
of the people's song.

THE ROLE OF THE CANTOR

The cantor
is responsible
for leading
the
musical
expression
of the people...the
assembly, choral
groups, solo singers, &
instrumentalists, among
whom organists have
been especially
important for Lutherans.

The cantor uses whatever musical
resources are available,
using them in a manner appropriate
to the talents of those serving and the
needs of the people who are served.

The cantor's work
is a worthy
service to God,
God's people,
and
the world.

The cantor leads
the earthly assembly
in a foretaste of
John's vision of the heavenly assembly
in which all creatures give
praise, honor, glory and power
to the Lamb.

—IT IS A HIGH AND HOLY CALLING—

A HIGH and HOLY CALLING

*Essays of Encouragement for the
Church and Its Musicians*

PAUL WESTERMEYER

FOREWORD BY
ZEBULON M. HIGHBEN

MorningStar
MUSIC PUBLISHERS *A division of
ECS Publishing Group*

MorningStar Music Publishers, Inc.
1727 Larkin Williams Road, Saint Louis, Missouri 63026-2024
morningstarmusic.com

© 2018 by MorningStar Music Publishers, Inc.
All rights reserved. Published 2015
Printed in the United States of America

No part of this publication may be reproduced, stored in a retrieval system, or transmitted, in any form or by any means, mechanical, electronic, recording, photocopying or otherwise, anywhere in the world, including public performance for profit, without the prior written permission of the above publisher of this book.

ISBN 978-0-944529-77-5

Library of Congress Control Number: 2017917218

Frontispiece: The Role of the Cantor © 2011 The Association of Lutheran Church Musicians (ALCM). Reprinted by permission. Copies of the color poster may be purchased from ALCM by calling 800-624-2526.

Part I reprinted with permission of *Pipenotes*.

Part II and Chapter 17 reprinted with permission of *The Hymn*.

Permission is granted to reprint "Music in the Service of the Gospel: Discerning the Church Musician's Vocation through the Life and Work of Paul Manz," *CrossAccent*, Spring 2017 (25:1): 5–13. Copyright © 2017, Association of Lutheran Church Musicians.

"The Lord Now Sends us Forth" English text by Gerhard Cartford copyright © 1996 Augsburg Fortress. Reproduced by permission.

"Tell all the truth but tell it slant" THE POEMS OF EMILY DICKINSON, edited by Thomas H. Johnson, Cambridge, Mass.: The Belknap Press of Harvard University Press, Copyright © 1951, 1955 by the President and Fellows of Harvard College. Copyright © renewed 1979, 1983 by the President and Fellows of Harvard College. Copyright © 1914, 1918, 1919, 1924, 1929, 1930, 1932, 1935, 1937, 1942, by Martha Dickinson Bianchi. Copyright © 1952, 1957, 1958, 1963, 1965, by Mary L. Hampson.

Editor: Caitlin Custer
Cover art: Neil Johnston. www.paintstew.com
Cover and book design: Kristen Schade

To the
Twin Cities Chapter of the
American Guild of Organists and its Board
with gratitude for the opportunity
to serve you as your Dean

❧

TABLE *of* CONTENTS

Foreword

A number of years ago, the Association of Lutheran Church Musicians produced a poster print titled "The Role of the Cantor." The print featured six statements, rendered in an attractive calligraphic script, that defined the work and worth of church musicians. At the time, the historical term *cantor* was not widely used in American Lutheran parishes. Part of the rationale behind the print was to help recover the term while reminding all church musicians of their vocation as leaders of the people's song, regardless of their individual titles or job descriptions. The title of this book, *A High and Holy Calling*, is taken from that print. It is an apt title, because it points directly to this volume's unifying theme: Church musicians have a vocation, and it is an important one.

Paul Westermeyer has been writing about the vocation of church musicians for almost as long as he has been writing. His first book was a practical guide to the nuts-and-bolts of the cantor's work: study, practice, employment, clergy-musician relationships, and knowing and capably serving the assembly.[1] His most recent book (prior to this one) reflected more deeply on the cantor's vocation, the history that shapes that vocation, and the current cultural and ecclesial challenges that church musicians face.[2] Between those two texts are myriad books and articles about other topics in church music—it is a rare church musician's library that does not include at least a few Westermeyer volumes—but it can rightly be said that a substantial part of Paul's vocation has been to remind church musicians of the value of their own.

Anyone who has worked for very long in the church in any capacity knows that such service brings abundant joy, but also sorrow and suffering. For twenty-first century church musicians, the suffering frequently includes disparagement of their calling: Music in worship is treated as decorative rather than substantive; culturally driven marketing concerns are prioritized over assembly song; and the church musician's expertise and experience are undervalued, both within the church and in outside

---

1. Westermeyer, *The Church Musician*.
2. Westermeyer, *Church Musicians: Reflections on Their Craft, Call, History, and Challenges*.

musical circles. Such denigration has become so ubiquitous that it is often not malevolent or personal; it is no less painful for that.

And this brings us to the present volume. *A High and Holy Calling* is really a devotional book. The topics of these brief essays vary widely, but woven through all of them like an ostinato or *leitmotif* is a profound sense of hope and gratitude for the work that church musicians do. This is Westermeyer at his most pastoral, offering a word of solace, support, and inspiration to those who make music in the church, no matter their contexts or circumstances.

To quote the author: "Be of good cheer." And read on, to be reminded once again of the worthiness of this good work, and the holiness of being called to do it.

Zebulon M. Highben

Preface

I did not intend to write this book. I was asked on a number of occasions, in response to lectures I gave or articles I wrote, whether I planned to publish them. Church musicians especially asked about this. One day I scanned some of this material and realized it had a common theme with an underlying assumption: that Christ's promise to sustain the church[1] is not about our attempts to prop up dying institutions. It's about trusting God to sustain the church, as promised, and then doing what we are called to do without fear. It's about the call to live out our vocations in our particular contexts. In the words of José Aguiar's hymn, translated by Gerhard Cartford,

> The Lord now sends us forth with hands to serve and give,
> to make of all the earth a better place to live.
> The angels are not sent into our world of pain.
> to do what we were meant to do in Jesus' name:
> That falls to you and me and all who are made free.
> Help us, O Lord, we pray, to do your will today. [2]

My assumption about Christ's promise had, I discovered, resulted in a common theme of perspective on and encouragement for the church and its musicians. That theme was not generated by my wishful thinking, but by God's promise. Whether our time is much different from any other time is an open question, but our time is certainly perplexing for church musicians who are under attack from often contradictory quarters and who are asking for help. I decided that it might be helpful to respond to their requests and see if a book could be fashioned as a resource for those in need of perspective or encouragement. Ours is a high and holy calling,[3] and we are wise to be reminded of that.

---

1. See Matthew 16:18 and 28:20.

2. This hymn appears in *Evangelical Lutheran Worship*, #538. There it is listed as "anonymous," but it was later found to be by José Aguiar. See Westermeyer, *Hymnal Companion to Evangelical Lutheran Worship*, 371.

3. "A high and holy calling" is from the last line of a poster titled "The Role of the Cantor" which some of us fashioned for the Association of Lutheran Church Musicians. See page ii.

The first twelve chapters are short reflections from columns I wrote as Dean of the Twin Cities Chapter of the American Guild of Organists, for the Chapter's monthly newsletter, *Pipenotes*. They are oriented toward organists. The next section of chapters about hymn performance is a set of four articles requested for *The Hymn*, the journal of the Hymn Society in the United States and Canada. Similarly, they are oriented toward organists, as well as anybody else who leads hymns, however they do it. The third section segues from hymns to vocation. The first of its chapters began as a plenary speech to the Hymn Society in the United States and Canada as it celebrated the five-hundredth anniversary of the Reformation. The next chapter was stimulated by questions I have had for a long time about J. S. Bach's *Clavierübung III*. The one after that began as a speech at Mount Olive Lutheran Church in Minneapolis, celebrating the legacy of Paul Manz. I edited all of these and added two more. I hope the result is a helpful book whose chapters can be read individually, in clusters, or as a whole.

I write as a Lutheran in the United States of America with a deeply ecumenical concern for the other parts and places of the church. I think that for there to be any genuine understanding and dialogue we have to work from our particular vantage points, though not uncritically, in view of the whole. We have to learn about and seek to understand the whole as best we can, but trying to be or represent what we are not leads us astray. I hope that what I say is helpful across the church, East and West. Those in traditions other than mine can apply it in their circumstances as I apply what they say in mine. I hope this contributes to the rich mosaic of the church.

Paul Westermeyer

I. REFLECTIONS

1

Communal Wisdom

The Twin Cities Chapter of the American Guild of Organists has regularly sponsored "organ crawls." These are visits to various churches to hear the resident organ played by a few organists, after which the listeners can get a closer look at the instrument and discuss what they heard. Fine players and playing, contrasting organs and spaces, and a variety of attendees characterize these occasions. The last component, a variety of attendees, needs to be highlighted. Organists and those with organ interests are usually present as would be expected, but so are congregational members of the churches and people from the surrounding neighborhoods who come from a number of vocational and other backgrounds. They may or may not be well acquainted with organs. This circumstance reminds me of an experience with just such people.

The committee at Ascension Lutheran Church, just outside Chicago, who called me to be their cantor, told me that the congregation did not sing very well. They asked if I could help. Yes, I said, I could do that. Then they told me that their organ was in bad shape (all too evident!) and asked if I could help them figure out what to do about it. I said I was not an organ virtuoso nor an organ expert, but I could provide them with resources and figure it out with them. The church formed a committee, I supplied them with data, and we went to work.[1]

It became obvious that we needed to hear various possibilities. So, I found churches in Chicago with contrasting organs from as wide a spectrum as possible, and we set out on organ crawls. The ground rules were

---

1. In 2016, the Twin Cities Chapter of the American Guild of Organists made a twenty-five-minute video to help churches engaged in projects of this kind. The video, *A Guide for Organ Committees,* tells the story of the Glatter-Götz/Rosales pipe organ at Augustana Lutheran Church in West St. Paul, Minnesota.

these: At each organ, I played exactly the same contrasting pieces and led the committee in singing exactly the same hymns. It was important that I—their normal organist—played, not a virtuoso who might try to sell them a particular organ, or otherwise add an extra variable. What happened when we removed these variables was interesting. Their requests that I tell them what to do receded. I had resisted their wishes that I figure this out for them and had told them that we needed to do it together. They began to discern differences in organs and what these differences might mean in their building, with their congregation, its singing, and its musical possibilities. The committee decided to buy a fine organ from an excellent builder which fit the space beautifully both in sight and sound, and represented very responsible stewardship of their resources.

That experience underlined what I had learned many times before: congregations are smart. They can choose a representative committee well. People with very little background in a given area can learn and discern well, hear well, and figure things out for the good of the whole. Organ crawls were central to this project—for normal human beings, not organ enthusiasts, giving falsehood to the notion that normal people don't like organs.

When I lead forums in churches, even about pretty obvious things, I often get this response: "Why didn't anybody tell us this before?" That, along with organ crawls and similar projects, suggests that we sell one another short. If we assemble all of the information we can, make it available to all of us, and work together with requisite checks and balances, we can do amazing things. Our life together, musically as well as otherwise, benefits from our shared communal wisdom.

2
People

Item: Organ crawls attract not only organ enthusiasts and musicians, but also people from surrounding neighborhoods, some of whom will tell you that they know little or nothing about music or organs.

Item: My brother-in-law, one of those who professes this lack of knowledge and who thinks he cannot sing at all, has on more than one occasion sent me a long article about organs from his local paper.

Item: I was recently at my seminary class reunion, sitting next to a former classmate (who became a very fine and faithful pastor) at a worship service. He did not sing a note, just as in chapel services when we were students.

Item: I know wonderful people in the churches I have served who did not sing.

Item: A former colleague with little to no musical training has collected many recordings of classical music.

All of these people understand and appreciate more about music and organs than they say they do. My brother-in-law asks intelligent questions. He once came to a choral concert I conducted, and afterward asked about a piece which he identified as "that piece which came around to the beginning again." He was hearing the music's form. The colleague with the record collection compares different interpretations of the same symphony with more insight than many musicians. My seminary classmate and most of the folks in churches who don't sing are appreciative of musicians and the music for which we are responsible. Sometimes their comments are more perceptive than they realize.

The people in the communities we serve include musical experts, people who know little about music in a formal sense, people who find music important, and people who find it unimportant. In the October 28, 2015, issue of *The Christian Century*, twelve people gave a wide spread of experiences related to "song." And, yes, some people have less appreciative points of view, like C. S. Lewis. He thought hymns were the gang songs of the church. Erik Routley characterized his position as having a "good shout."[1] People in Lewis's mold prefer spoken services called "Low Mass" in Roman Catholic circles, similar spoken services from the Book of Common Prayer among Episcopalians, less liturgical forms of worship where there is no music at all as in Ulrich Zwingli[2] in the Reformed stream, or the worship of Quakers which avoids all set forms other than silence and what individuals many feel compelled to say at the moment. All of these groups in their communal practice gradually but invariably seem to push toward a musical expression, but that does not deny the individuals who prefer silence and words without music. They are present in all of our communities. Their wisdom should not be overlooked or regarded pejoratively. They know intuitively—and by their attendance demonstrate—that spoken services are more musical in their communal, mnemonic, and proto-musical flow than services where music is used as an intrusive disruption or an assault on the purpose of a worshiping assembly.

This wide and colorful spectrum characterizes individuals who together make up the communities we serve. The culture presumes that everything is controlled by the analysis of how to win in a chosen category, such as in the common divisions by generation or taste or status or education or likes and dislikes. One of the problems with this presupposition is that people in our communities have a diverse array of age, likes, dislikes, knowledge, abilities, and appreciation—or not—of music. They don't match the flat and bland skew of our statistical analyses, agendas, or simplistic notions. This disjuncture is one of the things that continually reminds us of the way the church's music bubbles up against the grain of the culture's lack of concern for the neighbor. Music does not serve statistics, agendas, or simplistic ideas. It serves real people—delightfully!

---

1. Routley, "Correspondence with an Anglican Who Dislikes Hymns," 17.

2. Ulrich Zwingli (1484–1531) was a leader of the Reformation in Switzerland and the most musical of the sixteenth-century Reformers. Nevertheless, he abolished the historic worship of the church and all music—congregational singing, choirs, organs, and instruments of any kind.

3

Beauty, Hospitality, and Compassion

In the June 2014 issue of THE AMERICAN ORGANIST, the journal of the American Guild of Organists, National Chaplain Don Saliers reminded us that "in a culture of distraction, greed, and cruelty, the experience of beauty becomes essential to our humanity."[1] He had more in mind than the superficial sense by which we often define beauty. He cited Alejandro Garcia-Rívera's book *The Community of the Beautiful*, which describes a community of hospitality and compassion. This is related to what I once heard Saliers say about a children's choir that sang at worship. When he asked the children after the service what they liked about singing, one of them said, "It tastes so good." In his book *Bach: Music in the Castle of Heaven*, John Eliot Gardiner gets at matters like this when he says that Bach "makes it a great deal easier for us to focus on the injunction to love one's neighbor than on all the filth and horror of the world. We emerge from performing or listening to a Bach motet chastened, maybe, but more often elated, such is the cleansing power of the music."[2]

The beauty, hospitality, and compassion that these writers allude to do not happen without patience, persistence, and the long hours of composing and practice that are a constant companion for musicians and their craft. Organists spend large portions of their lives alone at organs in otherwise empty churches, perfecting their skills so that they can serve their communities as well as possible. Both parts of this rhythm are necessary—the time spent in solitude and the time spent in community. Solitude without community destructively turns in on itself by blocking the intrinsic nature of music to share. Community without disciplined preparation betrays the

---

1. Don Saliers, "Beauty, Holiness, and Everyday," 12.
2. Gardiner, *Bach: Music in the Castle of Heaven*, 478.

group by treating it poorly with music that never sings. Music itself, however, pushes toward a healthy symbiotic mix in both directions. And it ties beauty together with hospitality and compassion.

Our culture militates against both directions and against the union. It does not generate disciplined persistence except as it glorifies the self. It does not generate communal concerns because an individual "where's mine?" is the driver. And it highlights the celebrities so that those who do their jobs in service to their communities, out of the spotlight, are often made to feel pretty unimportant.

These issues, however we try to define or describe them (and they are finally indescribable and undefinable), nonetheless attend us all in all of our music-making. We are tempted to restrict them to certain composers or virtuosos or performances, when in fact they belong to all of us and to the communities we serve. When a fourth-grader sings a stunningly beautiful solo in an anthem and takes your breath away; when a clarinetist spins out a gorgeous descant above the choir; when the choir sings with a balance, tone color, and phrasing beyond anything you could possibly have expected; and when your hymn playing and the congregation's singing coalesce with a potency you had not anticipated, then what Saliers, García-Rivera, and Gardiner are reporting is palpable. It is present among us who are not the stars, but who are engaged in the weekly craft of music with our people.

We can't manufacture these moments, though they would not be there without our work. Nor should we try to manufacture them. Beauty, hospitality, and compassion are there without our forcing them. They are there in the quotidian—the daily, the usual, the customary—character of what we do. This is no small thing in our "culture of distraction, greed, and cruelty." We should celebrate it with our people in all of its understated wonder and grace.

4

Behind the Headlines

I recently wrote a biographical sketch about Johannes Riedel for the *Canterbury Dictionary of Hymnology*. Riedel taught at the University of Minnesota from 1953 until 1983. He directed the doctoral dissertations of fifty-eight graduate students in musicology, plus ten more in American Studies and English. He and his wife, Sophie Beuthner, escaped Nazi Germany, where he probably would have been a pianist and conductor. Instead, he became a musicologist and teacher in the United States, with a broad range of interests that included hymnody and church music. He had a world-wide reputation and twice received the University of Minnesota Distinguished Teacher Award of the Alumni Association of the College of Liberal Arts.

Soon after I finished Riedel's biography, I attended a funeral for Helen Billing at the Lutheran Church of the Resurrection in Roseville, Minnesota, of which I am a member. Helen played there for Lenten services and was the organist at churches in St. Paul and Park Rapids, Minnesota. She had thirteen children, ran a resort with her husband, Don, and was an avid organist and piano teacher with bachelor's and master's degrees in organ performance from the University of Minnesota. She wanted a number of large Bach organ works to be played at her funeral. Tim Strand, who knew her when he was the cantor at Resurrection, respected her wishes with a half-hour pre-service recital.

There are few references to Riedel now, twenty years after his death. He is one of the "famous men" who "perished as though they had never been."[1] His wife Sophie, though not as famous, was a respected teacher who has

---

1. Ecclesiasticus 44:1, 9.

similarly evaporated from our consciousness. I had a hard time even finding her birth date. Helen Billing is yet another example of such a person.

All of us know, have known, and know of these people. They were our teachers, preceded us, laid the groundwork for us, and did much that was both good and an influence for good. Their company includes not only the most visible people, but also behind-the-scenes organ builders and service persons who construct our organs and keep them working well. Not only musicians, experts in musical crafts, and those who "found out musical tunes"[2] are numbered among this group. It includes co-workers and the people who make our common life possible so that we can carry out our vocations as musicians, others can carry out their vocations, and all of us together can contribute our gifts to one another and to the common good. They have perished and will perish as though they had never been, but their works follow them.

Living in our armed camps—with their violent destruction of people and the planet and an accompanying absence of concern for the common good (testimony to what the church calls "original sin")—makes it easy to forget the good that has been done and that is still being done for and by us. I do not mean to minimize the horror of the paper's front page every morning or its posts in social media all day long. It is very real. But so is the hidden weal of people like the Riedels and Billing, which seldom makes the headlines. It is that weal which "sings as we go" (to paraphrase Pope Francis's encyclical),[3] stares down evil, and is the essential stuff of "life together."[4]

---

2. Ecclesiasticus 44:5.

3. Francis, *Laudate Si'*, 244.

4. Bonhoeffer, *Life Together*.

5

Bach and Reger

On the morning of March 19, 2016, on American Public Media, and in five live sessions that followed, Michael Barone, host and producer of the radio show *Pipedreams*, organized a J. S. Bach and Max Reger party that was an amazing festival of musical wonders. Here are some of my responses.

1. Church musicians are notorious for learning from one another in and across denominational and other divisions, in their time and across centuries and cultures. So Bach reached back to the music of Frescobaldi, organist at the Roman Catholic St. Peter's Basilica in Rome. In 1635, fifty years before Bach was born, Frescobaldi had published *Fiori Musicali*, a collection of pieces written for the Sunday Eucharist. In 1714, Bach performed them in Weimar, Germany, where he was the chamber musician and court organist at the Lutheran court and chapel. Over a century later Reger, a Roman Catholic organist, returned the favor. He learned from Bach, wrote music inspired by him, and has been called "a second Bach."

2. This learning across centuries, traditions, and cultures is not a theoretical detail. It points to the contrapuntal and harmonic lore stored in the music of composers like Bach and Reger. Behind that is the theological lore and the experience of those who hear this music. To paraphrase Barone in the *Pipedreams* broadcast the day after the festival, Bach's and Reger's music expresses intimate devotion and opens "cosmic portals." In short, music and its connections with thought and devotion have been learned through and forged in our history and experience.

3. Our star-studded culture hides what needs to be articulated. We are subtly and not so subtly acclimated to believe that the virtuoso composer and musician emerge from some isolated garret and are

the only musicians of value. The truth is that celebrating the work of the finest composers and musicians is very important. But there the truth ends. For example, great composers and musicians do not develop in isolation, nor are other musicians valueless.

Many competent persons in the list of supporting figures are little-known or unknown. Many musicians where we live and work are virtuosic and well-known, but a large number are quite competent and unknown. They include many of us, many of our students and teachers, plus families, church members, friends, and colleagues. Though our culture writes that group off, it is wise to remember what one of those unknown teachers told me when I was a very young student: The little-known musicians make the virtuosos possible.

Little-known musicians bolster, provide a network for, and often teach the most-gifted—who learn swiftly—when they are young; then the little-known carry out what their abilities and vocations make possible, learning from the most-gifted. Both groups take up the tasks they are assigned among the people they serve. That work has value for all of us well beyond what we are predisposed to think about it.

6

The Church's Song

Martin Luther spoke for most of the church across its whole history (yes, there are exceptions) when he said that music is a gift of God to be crafted as well as possible. The church's message propels that logic, which is why the church has created such a huge and unparalleled repertoire of splendid music. The congregational part of that repertoire is sung by people who, over long stretches of time, practice it by repetition but seldom rehearse it. The choral part is sung by people who, over long stretches of time, sing together and also rehearse. The congregational part has yielded some of the world's finest folk song, the choral part some of the world's finest choirs.

Since it is not fundamentally a musical organization, however, the church does not always sing well. Worship is related to all sorts of people who assemble for particular worship services. There are times when those people include few or no musicians, and maybe some monotones who also are welcome to the congregational party. There are times when the assembly is learning new things or is in the midst of turmoil. There are times when singing is under duress from both external and internal, conscious and unconscious sources. Like music itself, the church's song is not a static condition. Over the long haul, however, it transcends challenges and moves toward its intrinsic excellence.

There are challenges at various times and places on this overarching trend toward excellence. They come about through differences of opinion, which create tensions and disputes. They are momentary in the light of centuries, but they sometimes persist for lifetimes. At the end of one set of extremes is the highest possible quality of music defined musically. At the other end is music as a tool for things like pastoral care, ethics, or evangelism, with quality of music omitted or defined in ways extrinsic to music. At the end of another set of extremes is preserving the classical because it is seen as a past and present value. At the other end is opposition to the classical because it is seen as an irrelevant relic. In between these extremes are gradations and mixes derived from both the church and the culture. Distrust, fear, and wars exacerbate things and make snarly and confusing swirls.

Organists are often at the center of these swirls. Though they hold differences of opinion themselves yet talk to one another in organizations like the American Guild of Organists, they tend to be attacked as a group. They don't easily fit preconceived molds. They play instruments that are large and small, and they play music that includes both expansive multi-voiced textures and intimate accompaniments. They play free-standing pieces and pieces with many other instruments and ensembles, yoked to both choral and congregational singing. They learn that phrasing, breath, melodic contours, and all of music's facets relate to human health and shalom and what is well beyond the strictly musical (if there is such thing). They play all sorts of music from all sorts of cultural settings and backgrounds from around the world, including what is classical and what is not. They relate to very long historical expanses and link generations. They lead singing with an instrument that, in our culture and many other ones, has proven to work for it better than any other instrument or ensemble. This cross-generational singing is easy to attack when generations are seen as divisive units.

All of this means organists are particularly well positioned for perspective on our confusion and for help through it. This help grows from the historical vision organists have as their birthright, which sees squabbles and attacks as momentary. It requires putting aside defensiveness and doing our jobs. That is not easy, and cannot be interpreted to mean that we should be silent about injustices which are a systemic part of the way church musicians are treated. We need to speak honestly, yet compassionately, about the problems. Mostly, however, we need to do our jobs as well as possible in the midst of the swirl, and on behalf of the people whom we serve and those who will follow them. The future is not what the rhetoric of destruction says, some appearances notwithstanding. And the people we serve—the known and the unknown ones—turn out to be more grateful for our constructive work than we ever know.

7

Bach

A week before Bach's Birthday Bash, an event hosted by Michael Barone on March 21, 2015, in the Twin Cities, the Bach Society of Minnesota went to Central Lutheran Church in Winona, and performed Bach's *St. John Passion*. Central Lutheran and Erik Floan, its Director of Worship Music & Arts, organized a dinner on Saturday evening, the day before the Sunday afternoon performance. I was asked to speak about Bach and his setting of the *St. John Passion* at the dinner. I discussed Bach, his work in Leipzig as the cantor, and worship life in Leipzig, then focused on Bach's setting of the passion from the gospel of John. It emphasizes Christ's winning the battle over sin and death, whereas his better-known *St. Matthew Passion* emphasizes Christ's sacrifice.

The next morning, between the services, Erik and I led a follow-up forum. One woman asked about how Bach's music engages us. I said that Bach wrote music which engages us at a deep level, which is rare. In our culture, virtually all music is regarded as a tool to sell things. Bach's music, however, is doing something else and reaches beyond that superficial patina to essence. I added that the music of the church, with Bach and the organ as chief representatives, is the music Erik and I regularly encounter as church musicians in our study and practice. It puts us at odds with music as sales technique and makes us—along with Bach—easy targets.

A week earlier I had conducted Bach's Cantata No. 12 for a vespers service at Christ Church in Minneapolis. This cantata is a profound inter-weaving of cross and crown, a theme that had emerged both at the Bach festival and in conversations about church musicians around the same time. A few weeks before, I had corresponded with a bishop about our abuse of and systemic injustice against musicians. I pointed out that by avoiding the central issues we face, organists and church musicians become scapegoats. Then I learned about yet another faithful church musician who had been summarily and unjustly dismissed years ago, with the divisive results still doing their damage. After that I heard David Weiss, Theologian in Residence at Pilgrim Lutheran Church and an Instructor in Religion at Hamline University, perceptively explain that we have to tell the painful yet joyful truth to a culture in denial about its death.

You probably have encountered in your life such a series of seemingly unrelated—but, with all of their paradox—ultimately enlightening and related events. Organists are particularly alert to them because we are so easily attacked in our responsibility for providing music that tells the truth and refuses to treat people like slabs of flesh to be sold or manipulated by money changers in the temple. Such music treats people with honor and respect, but, because we all would prefer to accede to our addictions and avoid the subversively constructive health and life that Bach's music offers us, we are tilted toward resisting the offer.

Do not despair. If your vocation is like Bach's, you too are telling the truth for the common good and facing similar sorrows and joys.

8

The Best and Worst of Times

It may be that Charles Dickens, though writing about the year 1775, was referring to every year when he began *A Tale of Two Cities* with the words: "It was the best of times, it was the worst of times..." Best and worst certainly seem to refer to our period.

Let's start with some of the worst. In one of his columns in *Sightings*, the online commentary about religion run by the University of Chicago Divinity School, Martin Marty referred to a report from the American Council of Trustees and Alumni about the absence of history from our classrooms and then mentioned "multi-partisan chaos."[1] That mention reminded me of recent articles in which writers have noted that we live in an age of anger and rage. The absence of history reminded me of our period's version of book burning, as "experts" have admonished us to avoid all language above a fourth-grade level, and to excise from our use all words that have historical associations, like "hymns"—with the spoken or unspoken assumptions that we ignore complexity and reduce things to a sales pitch that increases the treasury. Then I remembered a conversation at a Hymn Society conference where a few of us were discussing how things historical were being obliterated. I said something about the relation of budgetary matters and money to such cuts. A wise and seasoned hymnologist responded: "This is not about money, Paul. It's about vision."

The organ, which has a very long history, is tied into the iconoclastic worst of our period. Attacks on and cuts of the organ are not unique to the instrument. They are part of a large cultural milieu in which "Where's mine?" controls us. It leads us to self-centered concerns about what I can get in the present moment for myself, not what might be helpful for the

---

1. Marty, "History-less Judgments."

long haul. That in turn leads us to write off what the past can teach us to help not only ourselves, but our neighbors and those who will follow us as well. The result is to ignore the long trajectories of the past's importance for the present and the future. Musically, this is about my likes and dislikes. While likes and dislikes are not necessarily bad things, when they become the control of the church's music there is trouble. Community becomes an aggregate of easily-manipulated individuals, each seeking his or her own gratifications with little or no place for historical communal insights that organs, for example, provide.

Now for some of the best. At the Hymn Society conference where we had the conversation about historical ties being obliterated, a college-age organist led the hymn singing very well from a fine organ. His skill and the organ itself reflected plenty of historical understanding and preparation lived into the present and the future. Organ committees still meet and inevitably discuss all sorts of broad historical and long-term issues to which the organ invariably leads them. And all the time, rather remarkable organs are being cared for, reworked, and built anew.

These best of contexts include oases of deep concern for the common good, of which organists are a part. They fill the land under the superficial sheen of stardom in churches, schools, and associations where vision is in rich supply. With them comes the beauty of art and music and concerns for the whole social fabric, the neighbor, and the planet.

Some years ago, an oasis was evident at the dedication of an organ in a seminary chapel. If I recall this correctly, one of the speakers was an organist who said something you would not expect an organist to say: that an organ is not about music. It's about the New Jerusalem. It's a little city that works together in love. You may have difficulty convincing an organ committee of that without the realization that omitting the musical piece is hyperbole that serves to highlight music's importance for others. Organ committees, along with thoughtful organists, choirs, and congregations, tend to discover the truth that it encapsulates. It and all the rest of the best of our period are worth remembering as we work in a maelstrom and are tempted to see only the worst.

Our mix of best and worst is not unique to our period. We, along with the organ, can contribute to the best in the midst of whatever worst we face.

9

Justice and Thanks

Consider the following.

1. In his L. P. Stone Lectures at Princeton Theological Seminary in 1926, Louis Benson, a minister and authority in hymnology, noted that seminary curricula omitted hymnody, leaving pastors unprepared for hymnic matters they would encounter.[1]

2. Almost a century later, it is still not unusual for pastors to report no study of worship, hymnody, or music in their seminary curricula.

3. Similarly, programs of study for musicians and teachers that integrate worship, theology, hymnody, and music are difficult to find.

4. A few schools have integrated these studies into fine programs, have received high marks for them, and have successfully prepared their graduates for work as musicians in churches and schools all over the world. In the last half-century, several of these schools have scuttled their programs for dubious reasons (Union Seminary, 1973; Southern Baptist Seminary, 2009; Luther Seminary, 2013).

5. Pastors and musicians learn their crafts in different schools and contexts, and they often have little or no knowledge of what the other is doing.

6. A power differential gives pastors control, though they often, by their own reporting, know less about music in worship than church musicians do.

---

1. See Benson, "Lecture One: The Apostolic Ideal of Hymnody," 15. Here Benson also notes hymnody's "place in the crowded ranks of theological disciplines that make for the preparation of the ministry of the gospel."

7. Our milieu teaches us that music is a matter of technical facility and that music as a discipline of study has nothing to contribute to a theological (or any serious) conversation. Music is perceived as a matter of superficial likes and dislikes to be used for whatever purposes you want. Since this view is so ubiquitous, both clergy and musicians easily and unconsciously gravitate to it.

These details reflect a system that shuts music out of theological study and results in unjust treatment of musicians. I hear about this at every conference I attend. Recently, a particularly egregious example of injustice to a very able and faithful church musician became, for me, the proverbial straw that broke the camel's back. This injustice stretched over many months during which I had been asked by groups completely unrelated to this debacle to address topics that included how musicians were treated. The coinciding of these two circumstances led me to conclude that somebody must say something about justice for musicians. I have tried to take this up in conferences, speeches, articles, and a previous book, *Church Musicians: Reflections on Their Call, Craft, History, and Challenges.*

In particular among musicians today, organists are especially vulnerable targets for attack and injustice. Why? Because the inherited musical wisdom of the church in both congregational and choral spheres is most evident in the study and practice of organists. Our culture does not like inherited communal wisdom, which is partly why we lash out at our neighbors so violently, organists among them.[2] This is a systemic issue. It is not only, or even primarily, about personality disputes. That knee jerk reflex, whether conscious or unconscious, is an attempt to avoid the substantive stuff we should be considering. In spite of the horrors we know about all too well, there are simultaneously incredibly positive but less well-known oases where pastors, musicians, and people work together extremely well on behalf of people in the surrounding community, and on behalf of one another. At the same time, there are organists in awful circumstances who somehow continue to do their jobs faithfully and well, no matter what.

I want to say here as strongly as possible that what needs to be said to organists, whatever their circumstances may be: thank you. This thanks extends to organists in individual jobs where communities of faith benefit from their work in all sorts of ways that permeate out from their central musical vocation. It also extends to the work organists do with one another. This is evident in chapters of the American Guild of Organists all over the

---

2. See Chapter 21 for more about organs and organists.

country, in all sorts of ways. Particularly noticeable is the work that is done planning and carrying out fine recitals, lectures, workshops, and worship services. It is also present in less obvious ways, as we learn from and work with one another whenever we need the help that our brothers and sisters supply so well. Thank you, thank you, thank you.

10
A High and Holy Calling

In July of 2015 Eileen Guenther and I gave two lectures on the topic of her book *Rivals or a Team? Clergy-Musician Relationships in the Twenty-First Century*. My part of the assignment was historical, providing examples of good relationships. It is not hard to find examples of bad relationships. But, though often hidden, the good ones do exist. Here are two examples of good relationships from the United States in the nineteenth century in this country.

Harriet Reynolds Krauth Spaeth lived at the center of a stimulating swirl of study among well-known men, among them her grandfather, father, and husband. Her son was Sigmund Spaeth, a twentieth-century musicologist who wrote about and composed music, hosted radio shows, and was a regular on the Metropolitan Opera Quiz. Harriet Spaeth did her own scholarly work. In 1868, when she was only twenty-three, she ably provided music from Germanic and English sources for the Lutheran *Church Book*, which, with her musical editing, was published as the *Church Book with Music* in 1872. In addition to her work on the *Church Book*, she translated German and Scandinavian hymns, and she was the organist for many years at St. Stephen's Lutheran Church in the vicinity of the University of Pennsylvania. She is hard to trace, partly because there is little history of St. Stephen's, partly because she was a nineteenth-century woman in the midst of well-known men, but mostly because she collaborated with others in her own good work, serving as a church organist without, as far as we know, a concern for how well she was or was not known. That humble outlook is what needs to be noted for perspective in our current day.

A contemporary of Spaeth and another little-known figure, William Benbow, came to Trinity Lutheran Church in Reading, Pennsylvania, as their Organist and Choirmaster in 1883, when he was 18. He stayed for thirty years and then went to Holy Trinity Lutheran Church in Buffalo, New York. He wrote hymn tunes, thought out what church music is about, and made this telling comment: "The experience of the centuries has proven that music having an easy and delightful swing and well-sugared is the kind that people will love most readily and afterward loathe most heartily."[1] It is hard to conceive of such a statement from someone who had not faithfully served people as a church musician in tandem with the clergy. That is exactly what he did, and he got high marks from the churches he served.

Benbow also illustrates the importance of teamwork across generations, before him and after him. Before him, for over a century until 1873, a Tannenberg organ was in use at Trinity in Reading. After him, his successor was Henry Seibert who studied with him, then with Pietro Yon, and then went to Holy Trinity Church in New York. Seibert's successor, Carroll Hartline, studied with Seibert, "thus beginning" what Brian K. Trupp, the author of the history of Trinity Church in Reading, called "the third generation of the 'Benbow' influence."[2] Fine musicians also followed Benbow at Holy Trinity in Buffalo, among them Roberta Bitgood and John Becker.

Take courage. We have some good mentors.

---

1. Benbow, "The Function of Music in the Service of the Church," 482.

2. Trupp, *A History of Trinity Lutheran Church 1751–2011*, 60.

11

Thoughts after a Widor Festival

In 2016, The Twin Cities Chapter of the American Guild of Organists held a festival in honor of composer Charles-Marie Widor. It was quite well planned and well executed, and John Near's[1] expertise helped us explore music Widor wrote which was not for the organ or not only for the organ. It opened up a world about which most organists, not to mention other musicians, have little to no idea.

That program introduced us to music which many of us might have known only vaguely, and which some of us did not know at all. We learned about Widor himself, his music, and the music of the period, giving valuable context to the performer and listener. If I heard the conversations rightly, opinions varied about the quality of Widor's whole oeuvre. Or, more accurately, there are varieties of opinions about different pieces, not unlike that variety for pieces of other composers. How we judge quality and what should or should not be in the repertoire is not what I want to emphasize, though that is an important conversation. What seems most important is what we learned about Widor's music, how that helps us with what we may play of it, and how that in turn helps to understand a broader musical terrain.

I don't know if there are composers of organ music who wrote for other instruments in an amount equivalent to Widor's. However, the breadth of what organists seem propelled to seek out, know about, and work at is surprising. I do not mean to say that this breadth is absent from other musicians. It is not. But this quality seems especially prevalent among organists. It not only refers to Bach, Widor, or other musicians from the past or from

---

1. John Near was the college organist at Principia College in Elsah, Illinois. His doctoral dissertation was a biography of Charles-Marie Widor.

cultures we usually know about and work in. Organists among us, both little known and well known, have made me realize this.

What has always struck me about organ teachers is that, though they may have been quite able teachers of organ technique, they are characterized by the added dimension of breadth. I suppose this may be just my experience, but I doubt it. It also seems to characterize organists as classroom teachers who know a lot about many topics. Organists seem constantly driven to historical and contemporaneous musical excursions, beyond just organ music. They are forever juxtaposing unlikely themes from various cultural sources, skillfully hiding them in polyphonic or homophonic textures, and knowing all along that they are leading us to a view of the whole musical waterfront.

Here is where this leads: A large body of not-so-visible music and thought stands behind *all* music. It may especially characterize organ music. This is probably no different today from what it has been in the past, but its potential for tension is heightened when the popular is valued at the expense of all the rest. What organists contribute to our common life does not live only at a popular level. What organists contribute gives us a breadth that goes beyond the popular and beyond organ music itself. It stimulates conversations, lectures, and educational ventures about other music and other topics near and beyond the organ.

Two examples were evident at a January 2016 program the Twin Cities Chapter of the American Guild of Organists sponsored. Kim Kasling, Professor of Music, University Organist, and Director of Liturgical Music Studies at St. John's University, provided a historical overview of organs in central Minnesota, which were largely influenced by the work of the Benedictines. His comments alluded to a larger historical and cultural breadth behind those organs. Soprano, organist, pianist, Dominican nun, and expert in Czech music, Anita Smisek, working with Czech and Czech/American organ music, showed us a comprehensive spectrum of music and a historical range well beyond the organ.

The bottom line is that the breadth of what lies underneath the Widor Toccata is a symbol for the breadth that lies behind what organists do. Be thankful and of good cheer. The human race not only needs, but desires— sometimes consciously, sometimes unconsciously, always for the long haul—the breadth of such support.

12

Legacy

When I drove back from the Institute of Liturgical Studies at Valparaiso University in Indiana after one of its conferences, I allowed enough time to make two stops. The first was at Elmhurst College in Illinois. Next to the main chapel at Elmhurst is a tiny prayer chapel. About forty years ago, when Naomi Rowley[1] and I were teaching there, we helped the college procure a very small one manual and pedal Brombaugh organ which is snuggled nicely into a corner of the prayer chapel. From time to time I have stopped to see how it is doing. This time, once again, it was the same as usual. It functioned perfectly, as if John Brombaugh had just installed it. I wrote to David Christiansen, who teaches organ at Elmhurst College, and asked him about it. He said that he loves the organ, then added, "…a good organ can hold its own."

The second stop was at Guardian Angels Catholic Church in Oakdale, Minnesota, soon after I crossed into Minnesota from Wisconsin. I've seen the nineteenth-century church building from Interstate 94 since I moved to Minnesota and have always wanted to stop and go inside. It was after 5:00 p.m. when I got there, and the church was locked. The large new church not visible from the highway was open, however, and the sexton was there. She had already locked up the old church, but graciously let me in to have a look. I was surprised to find it refurbished as an attractive small chapel in modern dress, where Mass is celebrated and weddings are held. I was even more surprised to find a Van Daalen organ there. After I got home I made some inquiries and found that the organ had belonged to a well-known Twin Cities organist, Diana Lee Lucker.

---

1. Dr. Naomi Rowley is a skilled church organist, organ teacher, and clinician. She is a graduate of Valparaiso University and Stanford University.

Organs like these that do not normally receive a lot of publicity dot the landscape. They include some fine instruments that have been built in our lifetimes and for which some of us are responsible in larger and smaller ways. Unless they are destroyed by neglect, natural disasters, fires, or vandalism, they will still be making delightful sounds long after we are gone. We are bequeathing a serious ecological crisis to those who follow us, as Pope Francis reminds us in his 2015 encyclical letter *Laudato Si'* (which we should note takes its title from his namesake's "Canticle of the Sun," best known in William Draper's English paraphrase "All Creatures of Our God and King."). I do not want to minimize that reality, but this also must be said: if the planet survives, we are bequeathing to our children's children and beyond some wonderful treasures, like these organs.

Though easy to overlook, this is no small thing. The finest craft that our ancestors have given us, as the organs they built, stimulates our creativity and evokes gratitude. Our ancestors also did some quite awful things, just as we do. We learn from them, too. Our responsibility, however, is not to work at the horrors, but together to craft the gifts we have been given as well as we can. These organs point to that craft and artistry in many ways. They are fundamentally musical instruments, of course, but they are much more. They pull together careful study, history, theory, math, technology, woodwork, metalwork, artistry, sound, piety, devotion, vocation, and craft for the neighbor into a set of communal resources that results in a small city of love that works together both in the building of the instruments and in the way they function. Amidst all that is less than salutary, we can ponder and give thanks for such remarkable treasures—as will those who follow us.

II. HYMNS

13

Perspective

Like all music, hymns are performed. Unlike much, if not most, music performed around us, hymn singing by worshipers does not exist for the purpose of listening to trained performers, live or recorded. On the contrary, hymns are performed in services of worship by people who are mostly untrained musicians.

Counter-cultural

This rather unique set of circumstances is counter-cultural and all too often avoided. When the culture calls the shots, "It's just a hymn" is a characteristic comment. People who say this are not bad people. They are simply conditioned by a culture that forms us to say things like that. Performances of classical or popular music by performers with flawless skills serve as our ideals. Worshiping assemblies do not fit these ideals.

Worshiping assemblies are composed of people who, by and large, have had little or no musical training. These assemblies may include monotones or persons with little formal education, or perhaps those with disabilities. Some do not match pitches well. Rhythms may confuse others, while still others may match pitches and get rhythms right but have no idea what singing in a group might mean. Since the cultural ideal for music is listening to flawless performances, often solo ones, our society teaches us not to sing unless we are trained singers. At the same time, it teaches trained musicians that hymn singing is meaningless or hopeless because it is done by people who are not musicians and who seldom, if ever, rehearse. The cultural presupposition is that all music is for listening, while the purpose of hymn singing is participation. Listening to hymns is not why they exist.

Consequences

"It's just a hymn" treats hymns like fillers which add or subtract time to a worship service. In this view, the meaning of text, music, or text and music together is not important. For reasons unrelated to meaning, stanzas may be added or subtracted either in planning or in a service on the spur of the moment. If this alters or avoids the hymn's meaning or structural integrity, so be it. The meaning of the text and the musical flow of the hymn are not important considerations.

Another consequence of "It's just a hymn" is to turn church musicians into functionaries with technical musical skills. Understanding why a congregation sings is not seen as important since music is regarded as a filler or maybe a virtuosic attraction, which is its own form of ancillary filler. When music is not considered integral to a worship service and is relegated to a functionary who happens to be necessary but has no substantive importance, hymns become increasingly irrelevant in a circle that feeds on itself in a downward spiral.

The Nature of Hymn Singing

Those who have some notion of the importance of hymn singing do not fit the picture I have just described. There are many more such people than our rhetoric often suggests, in spite of the obstacles these folks face. What I will say here is nothing new for such people. It needs to be said anyway, however, in a culture where it is seldom stated and where hymn singing often proceeds from an unexamined inertia. That inertia is not necessarily a bad thing, and points to the underlying importance of hymns, but, like all human activity which is worth doing, hymn singing and reasons for its being need to be examined and articulated.

1. **A hymn is an event in the flow of worship.** A hymn is an important occurrence in a service of worship, a happening. It is not an incidental intrusion or accidental occurrence. It means something, something important. Part of its importance is that, with the gift of music, it bears praise, prayer, proclamation, and story, usually in some mix in proportions that vary from tradition to tradition.

2. **A hymn is a *musical* event in the flow of worship.** Music is a gift of God that lives through time just as human beings live through time. Music orders time and is about the relationship of human beings to time on their journeys through life. Singing a hymn rather than speaking it is important. The texts of the Psalms and

hymns we sing are about all of life before God. The gift of music as an integral part of this event points to the pilgrim journey of the people of God for the glory of God on behalf of the neighbor. That is why this understanding of music—for the glory of God and the good of the neighbor—is the underpinning of the Psalms, Paul's comments in Colossians 3:16, and the understanding of music throughout the history of the church.

3. **As it is sung, a hymn passes through time and is gone.** The passage of music through time, in this case with singing to God for the neighbor, presumes active musical participation of specific people in specific times and places. It is tied to the larger cloud of witnesses who have gone before us and will come after us, to be sure, but in that overarching context it is local. It has never been voiced before and will never be voiced again in this particular way by this particular group of people in this particular time and space. It symbolizes and relates us to everything on the pilgrim journey from creation to consummation. It comes and goes.

4. **Leaders of hymns are called to use their ears.** The place where the singing is done may be the same week after week, so acoustics may essentially remain the same. But they are not the same as the acoustics of the church down the street or across town or across the world. The people week after week may be largely the same ones, but they change as visitors come, people die or move away, and new members join. The people present are in good or bad voice, healthy or sick, have experienced a funeral one week and a wedding the next. Seasons change. So do temperature, humidity, time of day, readings, themes, and sermons. There is little that does not vary, and even slight variations are significant. Musicians, whose job is to use their ears, are called to listen and to lead sensitively in all of our changing circumstances on the journey.

5. **All of the musical skills musicians practice and develop apply to hymn singing.** A hymn is not "just a hymn" any more than a concerto is "just a concerto" or a fugue is "just a fugue" or a song is "just a song." These are all music. A hymn is generally sung with a hymn tune, which is music. Music involves craft and skill which grow out of its raw material as the gift of God in the creation. Musicians are called to develop the attendant, implicit, and necessary craft and skills. That is their vocation. These need to be applied with as much attention and care among untrained singers

as they do among trained musicians. A hymn assumes the worth of human beings, all human beings. And all human beings— including ones who have been abused and cannot sing for a time or who are presumed to be tone-deaf or who have disabilities or little education or are illiterate—respond to musical pitches, phrases, rhythms, and musical structures. All of us can learn and are called to learn, not only trained musicians or any one class or stratum of society. That does not mean people in worshiping assemblies are called to be trained musicians. It means we all respond to musical stimuli and long to sing. Those of us who lead the singing are called to do it with musical sensitivity. When this is done, amazing things happen. We all learn to sing, find our voice, sing Sunday's hymns silently or aloud during the week, and find help in time of need—because to be human is to sing, especially with texts that are worthy of being voiced in worshiping communities.

6. **A hymn is live in the flow of worship.** Our capacity to record sounds has led to some wonderful things—like learning from specific performances or hearing music in various contexts and for various purposes. But a recording—any recording—cannot be used for hymn singing without destroying its purpose. Hymn singing is live. It is an event in which a particular community voices its praise, prayer, proclamation, and story in a particular time and place. It is not a recorded or canned activity. We can learn from live or recorded sounds by other people in other times and places, but they cannot substitute or be the ideal for our very particular sound in our very particular assembly in the moment.

7. **Hymn singing proceeds without amplification.** Hymn singing is by real people led by real voices or instruments, all in their natural states. It is wholly apart from unnatural magnification and synthesized sounds. It is profoundly honest.

Hymn singing gives us our voice. That is no small thing and certainly not "just a hymn."

14

Tempo

When I took the position of Cantor at Ascension Lutheran Church in Riverside, Illinois, just outside of Chicago, the pastor there was Paul Landahl. In the interview process Paul and I had agreed that we were going to meet at an appointed time each week to plan worship—reviewing the past Sunday or Sundays and then working as far ahead as we could—possibly for the whole church year. We never made it for a year, but we did manage to plan several church seasons ahead and then adjust things week by week.

I played the first service before we met, and the following week we got together as planned in a room of the church which housed Paul's theological library and a wide range of hymnals and liturgical resources. The first thing Paul said to me when we met was, "I didn't like the way you played that hymn." Paul and I had agreed that we were going to be honest with one another, and we each knew enough about the other's ego strength to realize that neither of us would collapse at such a statement. He probably expected me to say what I did say: "Why not?"

Paul is not a musician and did not use a musical vocabulary to articulate what was bothering him, though I think he used general terms like fast or slow. I gradually figured out that issues related to tempo were involved, but they were not only or exactly about fast or slow in a metronomic sense. After he explained his concern I explained what I had in mind, and then we discussed the hymn and how it fit the service. Week by week this kind of thing happened over and over. What also happened over and over is that each of us would often say something like, "Oh, I see," and then we might flip sides. It was wonderful.

In the process of our conversations I gradually began to think a bit differently about tempo. From the time I started playing for congregational singing in high school I had obviously thought about tempo, but my thoughts initially concerned each individual hymn as a unit. I had gradually expanded that to the whole service and how the hymn fit into it, but in the planning sessions with Paul Landahl this expanded into a still more comprehensive picture. Visiting other churches and visiting the students in the Master of Sacred Music program at Luther Seminary with St. Olaf College confirmed, deepened, and broadened this understanding. The following are some things I learned, including the fact that many sensitive church musicians know about these things and apply them in their craft, though they are seldom written down.

The Hymn

A hymn has its own tempo, related to the tune and the text it sets. This involves the kind of considerations musicians apply to any piece of music which allow the music to settle into a coherent flow, in this case involving a text as well. These considerations include the nature of the tune and the text, how they fit together, the reasons for being written and context in which they were written, the performance practice of the time and place when they were written (which may or may not be the same for text and music), details about particular notes, motives, and phrases, how they fit together, and the overall form and shape of the whole. As I will shortly indicate, all of this has to be applied to a very particular people in a very particular place here and now.

There is no single tempo that is the only solution. Every tune has a spectrum of possibilities within a range, and every text bears on this range. WER NUR DEN LIEBEN GOTT, for example, can work well either a bit slower with the pulse defined by each beat, or a bit faster by three beats as a unit, so long as this range is not extended too far to result in dragging or in rushing. What that means, of course, will differ from musician to musician just as all musical performances differ from performer to performer. Part of the task and responsibility of musicians is to translate the notes on the page or in the memory bank into sounds that hang together meaningfully. One solution does not fit all.

The Congregation

The hymn and tune do not exist in a vacuum of performance practice from a past time, whether yesterday or three centuries ago, or in any other kind of isolation. Historical details are important, but the hymn and tune finally sound with a very specific group of human beings at this moment. Many things about this group relate to tempo.

The group has a history which bears on the moment. This history may stretch across generations for a church and may be much shorter, as in a group that meets only once. It relates to events in the group's or the wider society's experience—a tragedy, a jubilant celebration, both or neither, from the recent past or of signal importance from long ago. It includes a language or languages from one or more ethnic identities. All of this relates to tempo. Historical issues have strong ongoing influences in the present.

The hymn is sung in a space. A space has acoustical properties such as carpeting or hard surfaces, which do or do not reflect sound. Acoustics are critical, sometimes more important than anything else for tempo.

Additional factors include these: seasons of the church year; other religious themes; seasons of solar and lunar time; hot or cold; humidity; open or closed windows; outside sounds or their absence; sickness, health, size, and age of the assembly; and the visual and architectural setting.

Sensitive musicians are wise to analyze all of this, but mostly they respond in the moment by their ears. The sensitive musician listens. Students of John Ferguson[1] have this listening in mind when they say "Ferguson negotiates with the congregation." Again, there is no single precisely correct solution, but a range within which a correct possibility lies.

The Service

You may have experienced a worship service where something did not seem quite right. If you thought about it, you may have discovered that it rushed, or it dragged, or the pastor and the musician were at odds so that dragging and rushing gave confusingly mixed signals.

The overall issue here is pacing. A given service has a fitting pace. A congregation has a characteristic pace. A given pastor and a given musician, as well as lay assistants who lead by word or gesture or movement, have characteristic paces. For a service to flow coherently a communal sense of pacing has to emerge. This largely happens unconsciously, but church musicians are the ones who most consciously figure it out. Elements like the following have to be considered by the musician who leads the assembly in its singing.

---

1. John Ferguson is Professor Emeritus of Organ and Church Music at St. Olaf College, and a composer and expert in leading congregational song.

Where does the hymn come in the service? Beginning, end, in connection with words, in connection with communion? If there is a psalm, is it a metrical setting? If not, how is it constructed—with a congregational refrain, chanted by the whole assembly, both of these, neither? If there is a service setting, what is it? How do all of the musical events relate? Each of them has its own tempo, but that tempo relates to all of the others. There is a high-level rhythm to even the shortest service, with a single hymn as the only musical event. Multiple musical events give the high-level rhythm a musical cast that includes keys. The absence of a key contrast, for example, can harm a narrative counterpoint of themes, however, utilizing a key contrast can help to exegete it.

How does the presider pace the service? Is it deliberate, accidental, impulsive, fast, slow? This relates to speech as well as to gesture and movement, and it includes how fast or slow readers read. Is there nervous energy, a sense of calm and clarity, or a need to just get through it? Pastors and musicians may be able to talk to one another about these things, as Paul Landahl and I did. If that is not possible, however, musicians have to adjust. What that means is not easy to describe. The best solution may be the same as or different from the presider, or both, changing as necessary.

The Musician

The vocation of the church musician, more than of any other leader at worship, has to take all of this into account and live it out responsibly—that is, thoughtfully and with practice. Tempos of hymns and other singing that musicians lead are among the most decisive factors that control whether or not members of congregations participate in worship. Musicians often are destructive, not helpful. The world's idea that "it's just a hymn" leads some musicians who play in churches to execute extremely well-practiced preludes and postludes, but to sight-read hymns meaninglessly with no understanding of the damage they are causing, or the good they could bring. Fortunately, there are some wonderful church musicians who take their roles seriously and serve as examples, working these things out for the glory of God and the good of the neighbor.

15

Breath

Communal Song

George Black, a past president of the Hymn Society, once said that a community of love will sing together, that to tamper with the people's prayer is a tricky business, and that the leader of the people's song needs to take some risks, like sometimes letting the people set their own tempo. I have learned how profound Black's insight is by listening to congregations when they are not only left to set their own tempo, but allowed to sing together as their individual voices form an expressive community whose praise, prayer, proclamation, and story take wing. This realization is underlined every time I visit a congregation who valiantly attempts to sing despite the destructive roadblocks leaders of the song throw in their way. This destruction usually has little or nothing to do with leaders' overall technical facility. It has to do with leaders' failure to understand breath, particularly the breath of a congregation.

An Instrumental Conception

The destruction is in part driven by our cultural presupposition that music, at its core, is instrumental, not vocal. That is true even when the voice is highlighted. An instrumental conception almost always serves as the underlay, and seldom—apart from some congregations and choirs—does the vocal stand alone or supply the conceptional framework.

I was recently present at a meeting of a number of people from various churches who, as part of the day's activities, had a brief worship service which included a hymn. The leader of the service said, "We have no music today, so we'll have to do this..." and started to sing with wrong intervals and a wrong rhythm that the community quickly corrected, took over, and sang on its own. That illustrates not only how well a community can sing on its own—which I had learned long ago, in high school, when I was shocked to hear a congregation grab hold of its singing despite a thoroughly incompetent musician—but also how communal singing is not perceived as music. "We have no music today" meant "We have no instrumentalist." Communal vocal sounds, culturally-speaking, are not regarded as music. The results of this perspective are devastating.

The Results

Most of our singing is led by instruments. When instrumental leaders presume an instrumental conception, several things happen.

1. The tempo is whatever feels right for the fingers, which is usually faster than communal song demands.

2. As the singing proceeds, the instrumentalist often goes faster, making it increasingly difficult for the congregation to keep up.

3. If the organ is being used, there is no lift between phrases so that sounds drone on continuously for a whole stanza at a time.

4. If a piano is being used, longer notes in the melody are perpetually filled with arpeggiation so that communal sustenance is hidden or obliterated.

5. The beat increases in speed at cadences with no sense of the flow of phrases.

6. The space between stanzas is metronomic, or the speed of the beat is increased as at phrase endings.

7. If an instrumental group is leading, its own sound, sometimes amplified, often becomes a preoccupation and all that can be heard, so that listening and responding to the singing group itself—who presumably is the most important group in this activity—become impossible. Organists sometimes do the very same thing, as do vocalists through microphones. In all of these cases, congregational singing suffers and may be destroyed altogether.

8. Since the people in our culture no longer sing, sometimes the presupposition is that we should sing for them—which turns out to mean we should play for them. Then the church has simply collapsed into the culture, which in fact longs to sing. Not to help them realize that longing is a dreadful solution.

Good instrumentalists will tell us that most of the instrumental misdeeds are simply poor music-making, and that many instrumentalists perform with understanding and nuance that elevates the experience and encourages singing when it is present. That is true, and it should be noted that church musicians who have studied theological, musical, and liturgical subjects tend to be best suited to these circumstances. The church's unfortunate systemic penchant in this country is to shut out both the finest music-making and especially to shut out musicians from any theological dialogue, and then to use them as scapegoats when problems arise.

All of this leads to bad congregational singing or no congregational singing at all. It forces congregations into, at best, shallow breaths with no reserve and no shalom or resonance. Texts become meaningless vocables through which people fight to stay afloat. Narratives lose their coherence, prayer loses its entreaty, proclamation loses its prophetic punch, and praise loses its jubilation. The congregations who sing in spite of these roadblocks continue to amaze me, though some congregations, no matter how valiant, lose the battle. In either case, congregational song suffers.

Ruach and Music

It does not take much biblical study to discover how important the *ruach* is—a Hebrew word, which in Greek becomes *pneuma*, and in English, *spirit*. *Ruach* refers to the breath or wind of God, tied to the breath or wind of humanity which God gives us. It is about the principle without which there is no life. Singers, who may or may not know anything about this biblical understanding, learn very quickly how important breath is and how connected it is to life. Their teachers continually say things like: "sing on the breath," "take a deep breath," "take a life-cleansing breath," "sing that whole phrase in one breath," "breathe here," "breathe there," "you need a good breath for this phrase the same as you need a good breath to live." Good instrumental teachers do exactly the same thing when they say things like: "make the piece breathe," "take a breath between those phrases," "hands off the instrument, and sing that line with a breath," "give the piece some breath, and let it live."

On the Breath

An assembly which sings well lives on the breath as the individual voices ride on columns of wind. If a leader does not realize this, bodies and their wind supplies become disengaged, and the singing collapses into a superficial gloss that never gets to the breadth of human life or its reality. An assembly of the church that gets blocked in its singing is blocked from the life force that relates to God and God's gifts. This profound overall reality turns out to have quite specific musical features. It is these features that leaders who want to help people sing need to figure out.

1. Between stanzas of a hymn there needs to be time for a breath— and for swallowing—as Robert Baker[1] told the Master of Sacred Music students at Union Theological Seminary. Precisely how this is handled may well be different from one leader to another, but if this consideration is omitted, there is trouble—deep trouble.

2. The tempo of communal song has many variables (as indicated in Chapter 14), and breath is associated with all of them. If breathing is truncated or squashed in some way, the tempo may or may not be the problem. But trying to determine a tempo with no sense of the breath a given hymn requires is an exercise in futility.

3. The tempo of communal song may not be the tempo of an individual soloist, be that soloist a vocalist or an instrumentalist. The tempo of communal song may not be the tempo of an instrumental ensemble. In either of these cases the nature of the breath is a critical consideration, and the nature of the performing medium is a critical component.

4. Different hymn tunes require not only different tempos, but different kinds of breaths. A tune with a prophetic punch at the beginning of the line is not the same as one pulled forward with a teleological tug from the end of the line. Texts with their theological meanings have similar characteristics. Praise and proclamation are likely to get an initial prophetic punch, like with "A Mighty Fortress." Prayer is pulled forward with a teleological tug, like with "O Splendor of God's Glory Bright."

To read about this topic may seem theoretical and unimportant, but to visit a community that sings and then to visit one where singing limps along or is absent demonstrates without any words how critical this is. The oases of the church where people sing and have sung for the past two thousand years are some of the church's deepest treasures for which we need to give thanks.

---

1. Robert Baker was the Director of the School of Sacred Music at Union Theological Seminary in New York City, a skilled organist and organ teacher.

16

Texts and Music

Hymns, Tunes, and Settings

A hymn is a text—words. Words are very important. In the Christian view, as the prologue to John's gospel says, in the beginning was the Word, which became flesh. So it is not without reason that composers of hymn tunes seek to make their tunes fit and express the words. And it is not without reason that wise church musicians who lead hymns begin by understanding the words and their meaning, and then they seek to make the musical settings of the texts spin out from and break open the meanings of those words. They do this both for introductions to hymns as these prepare for the singing, and they do this throughout entire hymns as they unfold.

There is no one-size-fits-all way to do this. Those of us with modest abilities can do it as can the virtuosos among us. It can be done quite simply, and it can be done with all of the musical complexity one can possibly imagine. In any case it can be done well or poorly, constructively or destructively. Music can get in the way, or it can be what Mary Louise Bringle[1] insightfully calls translucent to the text. Words bear on tempo, volume, phrasing, pitch, articulation, breath—that is, all of the aspects of music that musicians learn about in their study and training.

Words of hymns grow out of different linguistic and ethnic contexts. These words and the way they are put together relate to the ways a given group of people moves and communicates, which has both rhythmic and melodic dimensions. The tunes of hymns therefore differ not only within one linguistic or ethnic tradition, but from language to language and

---

1. Mary Louise Bringle is Professor of Philosophy, Religion, and French, and Chair of the Humanities Division at Brevard College in North Carolina, as well as a very able and perceptive hymn writer.

ethnicity to ethnicity. A Swahili text will not propel a tune in the same way that a Japanese text or a French or a German one will. Translations add another layer to this mix. For example, a Japanese tune with a Japanese text translated into English poses challenging questions. If the tune presumes a simple unison line with little or no instrumental participation, in an English-speaking context where four-part instrumental harmonizations are common, what will you do if you are leading the singing? How will you handle a hymn tune from a culture with musical expectations that are quite different from the one you are serving?

The questions continue. What will you do with an African American spiritual in a white context or a white nineteenth-century English tune in an African American context? How does racism rear its ugly head and not only cause hatred and injustice, but interfere with music? What is the most just and hospitable musical solution at the moment and over the long haul? What about a Norwegian context in which a substantial Hmong population is present? What happens musically at the beginning of this togetherness, and what happens over the long haul?

Musicians characteristically hear various sounds from various times and places and then say, "What if we put these together?" From there, they usually propose a juxtaposition or transformation. Musicians are very important in this process because, in their practice with their ears, they process the music they experience from the past and the present and give the lie to any position that says there is only one possible style. The notion of one style generally forces a known tradition to be regarded as sacred and the only right one. Or, conversely, it forces an unknown tradition to assault the known and to be regarded as the only one that is ethical. These are not unknown dilemmas when authorities uninformed about music tell us they have the answers and the only musical way.

Musicians who are responsible for leading hymns have to think out the various dimensions of a hymn and its music. As they do this, several things become clear. The first concerns the space where hymns are sung. Many of our churches are heavily carpeted and not well suited to singing congregations. In these spaces both words and music get eaten up as if they were in cotton boxes. Second, amplification is ubiquitous and sold as a fix for all such acoustical problems. Words and music then often get mashed into a meaningless sonic maze. Third, the amplification grows out of our musical presupposition that music is fundamentally instrumental and not vocal. Fourth, congregational singing has most often been done by voices alone, as is its very nature, even though our practice tends to forget or deny that. This means a voice or voices are best to lead it. Fifth, our cultural context tends to force foreign instrumental and amplified control on a hymn's intrinsic vocal nature. Loss of words, music, and the congregation's singing is the result.

Two clarifications immediately need to be made. First, judicious amplification which does not crash into and destroy the singers, can, in some limited ways, be helpful when the sound is naturally, not artificially, magnified. In churches that absorb sound like cotton boxes and are already artificially absorptive, limited amplification which does not call attention to itself can help on occasion. Second, organists are able to do amazing things that, in spite of our cultural roadblocks, can lead communal singing very well. There are two reasons for this. One is that organists have pipes, wind, and an ensemble with invariable imperfections at their disposal, and they can make sustained and staccato lines. This is all exactly like a community of voices who sing together. The other reason is that organists have the longest history of an instrumental relationship to congregational singing, and they can draw on its wisdom in various ways to help.

Sound

That different languages have different sounds, rhythms, and accents is obvious. What may be less obvious is that these have a bearing on the melodies that go with the texts of these languages. There is the still less obvious component of sound itself.

My children and grandchildren, most recently my granddaughter Naomi, have taught me over and over that sounds come before words and that a deep well of meaning is present in the sounds long before the words are there. Naomi, long before she was even two years old, had all sorts of inflections in her voice. Through these she expressed phrases that communicated questions, answers, exclamations, and commentary. Joined with gesture through dance or ceremony, these sounds communicated quite well.

Thomas Troeger[2] pointed to this reality when he said that he knows the nature of a phone call from the sound of the voice in the greeting before words about a given subject are present.[3] Martin Luther made a similar point when he referred to the nightingale as the "queen of all" to whom "with

---

2. Thomas Troeger is Professor Emeritus of Christian Communication at the Yale Institute of Sacred Music and a perceptive writer of hymns, as well as books about hymns, preaching, poetry, and music.

3. Troeger, *Wonder Reborn*, 88.

right good song and tuneful trill" we give thanks for "music so charmingly gay," though the "thanks [go] first to God, our Lord, who created her."[4]

To realize that meaningful sound precedes words is not our normal instinct. We are conditioned to think that meaning is a completely rational reality that can be comprehended only in our words. But, as Troeger says, for all of the "astounding things...that language can accomplish, it is still a net filled with holes, and there are vast currents of existence that it will never catch."[5] We think, for example, that we can translate a poem into prose to get the meaning precisely correct, but without the structure and rhythm of the poetry, the meaning itself is diminished. Even with a poetic translation the original sound is missing and with it a whole world of meaning.

So what? Luther helps us here. When he waxes eloquent about God's gift of music and how we are to craft it to let its essence out, the reader can sometimes get the impression that music is parallel to words in their proclamation, that music could proclaim the gospel on its own. But Luther is the last person to deny the importance of words and that the Word became flesh. What he is getting at is the close tie between words and sound, which is why, in the preface to Georg Rhau's *Symphoniae iucundae*, he makes the point that "the fathers and prophets wanted nothing else to be associated with the Word of God as music."[6] Sound is tied in the creation to words and music.

Or, as Troeger explains, we need not only a theology of the Word. We need "'a theology of sighing'" as well, "a theology of sound that is made by grief too overwhelming to speak, by grace too extravagant to name, by beauty too intense to articulate, and by prayer too profound for our lips to shape into speech...with 'sighs too deep for words.'"[7] The texts and music of our hymns, taken together in the event of a hymn's performance, disclose a remarkable mystery in the astounding things that words and sounds can accomplish; in the rational meaning of the words; in the music that sets them; in the grief, grace, beauty, and prayer of the sighs too deep for them; and in the whole that is more than the sum of its parts.

---

4. Luther, "A Preface for All Good Hymnals," 320.

5. Troeger, *Wonder Reborn*, 88.

6. Luther, "Preface to Georg Rhau's *Symphoniae iucundae*," 323.

7. Troeger, *Wonder Reborn*, 88.

III. VOCATION

17

Music and the Reformation: An Ecumenical Achievement

Martin Luther

As is well known, Martin Luther had a great deal of respect for the music of Josquin des Prez, an important Franco-Flemish Roman Catholic composer about thirty years his senior. The best-known quotation about Josquin from Luther is probably this one which comes from his "Table Talk" on December 14, 1531, ten years after Josquin died.

> What is law doesn't make progress, but what is gospel does. God has preached the gospel through music, too, as may be seen in Josquin, all of whose compositions flow freely, gaily, and cheerfully, are not forced or cramped by rules, and are like the song of the finch.[1]

I take it Luther meant what fine composers and improvisers inevitably discover, that knowing and using the rules well yields freedom, not bondage—parallel to following the Ten Commandments which Luther discusses in his *Small Catechism*.

Almost a century later, from 1609 to 1612, Heinrich Schütz, a Lutheran composer in Dresden, studied with Giovanni Gabrieli, a Roman Catholic musician at St. Mark's in Venice. As was mentioned earlier in Chapter 5, about a century after that, in 1714, J. S. Bach, as the chamber musician and court organist at the Lutheran court and chapel in Weimar, played the *Fiori Musicali* of Girolamo Frescobaldi, who had published this collection of organ music in 1635 for the Sunday Eucharists at St. Peter's Basilica in Rome where he was the organist. Those three examples—from the sixteenth, seventeenth, and eighteenth centuries—give the lie to the modern

---

1. Luther, *Luther's Works*, 128–130.

urban legends about Luther and about those who followed him.[2] The modern urban legends go something like this.

Everybody knows…

- that Martin Luther set out to break away from Catholic practices and beliefs,
- that he was the first person to introduce congregational singing into the church,
- that he stole his hymn tunes from bars, and
- that he thought the devil had all the good tunes.

In short, Luther is popularly seen both in and out of the church as an iconoclast and a lone ranger who started the church's congregational hymn singing, and who set out to junk everything the church catholic had bequeathed to the sixteenth century in order to start from scratch with music in bars. Nothing could be further from the truth than these stories that have become so commonplace in modern time.

The facts go something like this. The sixteenth-century church received a catholic heritage that stretched from the Bible onward. It included biblical readings, psalms, canticles, what Paul in Colossians 3:16 called "psalms, hymns, and spiritual songs," responsorial psalmody between biblical readings, hymnic poetry, and music to go with all of that. It also received sequences, sometimes with texts that stimulated more hymns and tunes, polyphony and the choral music that came with it, vernacular hymns like *Leisen*, the beginnings of music for the organ, and the Mass and Prayer Offices to which all of this related and which were all song. This is a wealth of congregational and choral texts and music, directly related to the worship of the church from many generations before the sixteenth century.

Along with this musical feast came thought about music from writers like Augustine and Boethius. This is less well known than the main course itself and seldom encountered in seminary curricula, though it is as instructive for us as the theological themes on which it bears and that are equally as complicated on their own. Erik Routley is one writer who attempted to examine some of this for those who are not technical experts, as can be seen in his book *The Church and Music: An Enquiry into the History, the Nature, and the Scope of Christian Judgment on Music*. Conversely, James McKinnon is among those who have examined it with more technical detail, as in his

---

2. Some of this is repeated in Chapter 19. It bears repeating in the two contexts, so I have included it in both places.

book *The Temple, the Church Fathers, and Early Western Chant*. Routley
was an English Congregational minister who taught at Westminster Choir
College, and was one of the twentieth century's most important hymnol-
ogists. McKinnon was a church organist and musicologist who studied at
Columbia University and taught at the State University of New York in
Buffalo and at the University of North Carolina in Chapel Hill.

There *were* sixteenth-century reformers who tried to avoid all of this
and others who severely restricted it. But Martin Luther was not one of
them. He gratefully received what he inherited. Like the church which
came before him, he used it and developed it. So did those who followed
him. For example, Luther and Lutherans kept the Mass, editing it as the
church had been doing for centuries. Lutherans kept more sequences than
the Council of Trent. They used Gregorian chant and *Leisen*, from which
they developed chorales. For the last five hundred years Lutherans have
sung and played a huge repertoire of congregational, choral, and instrumental music for the worship of the church. They have edited it, written
it, gratefully received it, and used it from others across the entire church
catholic. Any suggestion that we can get into God's presence by what we do
was excised (technically known as works' righteousness), but that was not
Luther's idiosyncratic notion. He discovered justification by grace through
faith in the Bible and in the theology of the church. He considered it a central part of the Christian faith from which the church in the sixteenth century had departed.

Hymns

Those who are concerned about hymns are likely to know all of this,
but it needs to be stated since it is so often hidden by the notion of Luther
as lone ranger and iconoclast. The Hymn Society in the United States and
Canada, a group whose central concern is hymns, reveals a corollary about
hymnody. I discovered it early on in my life when I started talking with
church musicians and then later started going to conferences of groups
like the Hymn Society. I learned that what Erik Routley is credited with
saying is true: "Church musicians are denominationally promiscuous."[3]
Church musicians actually talk to each other across denominational and
confessional divides, they work together and learn from one another, they

---

3. Though this does not seem to appear in Routley's writings, James Brumm—pastor, Director of
the Reformed Church Center at New Brunswick Theological Seminary, hymn writer, and author—
reports that he heard Routley say it in a class at Westminster Choir College during the first week of
September in 1980.

study texts and music from traditions other than their own, and they serve churches other than the ones they may have grown up in or whose confessional positions they embrace. They often remain committed to their own group's confessional postures, but still make these other contacts and maintain these other relationships.

This is no accident. Martin Luther, in his respect for Josquin, and for the church's musicians whom he consulted for help, simply reflected what church musicians do and what the church expects from them. If you want to see what the church expects from its musicians, just look at the church's hymnody. Go to virtually any denominational hymnal, or any library of choral music, or any oral tradition, or any set of digital resources. There you will find an ecumenical repertoire. The church itself is poetically and musically promiscuous. It does not restrict its song only to poets and musicians in a particular confessional stream. Instead the church lays hold of a remarkable catholic textual and musical whole. Musicians have simply worked out what the church does naturally and what it expects in its song in spite of itself.

If you happen to find a place where one narrow voice has silenced or sought to silence all the rest—which is hard to find, because it's hard to do—you know there is trouble. That kind of iconoclasm, even if limited, is inevitably resisted, if not immediately, then in the next generations. For example, Ulrich Zwingli's Great Purification of 1524 silenced the church in Zurich, but by the end of the sixteenth century Zwinglians there were singing Psalms. Anabaptists at first followed Zwingli's practice, but then sang martyr ballads and created the *Ausbund* of 1583, the oldest hymnal still in use. English Baptists did not sing at first, but Benjamin Keach argued the case for hymns in 1691 in *The Breach Repair'd in God's Worship*. Now Baptists are among the finest hymnologists. John Calvin restricted the church's singing to *a cappella* metrical psalms in unison by congregations only, but Reformed groups like Presbyterians now sing hymns, have organs and choirs, and use counterpoint and harmony. Lutherans, Calvinists, Zwinglians, Baptists, and many Anabaptists now use the same wide array of musical possibilities to which the church gravitates. The 1861 *Hymns Ancient and Modern*, the model of a modern hymnal, illustrates this mix. It was generated by Anglicans who at first had an aversion to hymns because of emotive excess among hymn singing groups like Methodists, but they discovered hymnody's catholic roots and gravitated to the whole. Charles Wesley's hymns, the center of the Methodist's singing, have not only influenced Anglicans strongly, but the entire church in the West.

There is nothing surprising here because the church invariably discovers that health requires a balanced diet, and "new occasions teach new duties."[4] No single source we construct provides enough nutrition from the whole diet God provides for us through our sisters and brothers in Christ, either for our journeys or for the journeys of following generations. The church naturally expects what its hymnals provide, in spite of itself.

Celebrations of the Reformation

The phrase "in spite of itself" needs some unpacking. Dirk Lange, a professor at Luther Seminary, was one of the planners of the five-hundredth anniversary of the Reformation celebration in 2017 in Lund, Sweden, in which Pope Francis participated. Lange gave presentations about that celebration in which he regularly referred to the one-hundredth anniversary celebration of the Reformation in 1617. He showed a woodcut in which Luther is writing his Ninety-Five Theses on the All Saints' Church door in Wittenberg, using a very long pen which extends far behind him. The Pope is there, and the end of the pen is knocking off his crown.

That fanciful depiction, though historically false, is unfortunately not so fanciful in the battle it pictures between Luther and the Pope—and then especially in what it implies about Lutherans and Catholics in the following centuries. As Lange pointed out, in 1618, the very next year after the one-hundredth anniversary celebration of the Reformation, long after Luther and Pope Leo X were dead,[5] the devastating Thirty Years' War began. That war was not caused only by Lutherans and Roman Catholics with their ugly and divisive behavior, to be sure. It was also caused by states and involved battles of political domination, control, and money. The church, however, in allowing itself to collapse into extrinsic battles and ingrown selfishness, helped set in motion not only its own divisions and warfare, but also contributed to the massive destruction, famine, and disease that the Thirty Years' War caused.

---

4. This line comes from the hymn "Once to Every Man and Nation" by James Russell Lowell. Though it can be read as progressive revelation that dismisses the once-for-all character of Jesus' life and death, it also can be understood to mean following in Jesus' unique footsteps as each age presents its own challenges.

5. Leo X's bull in 1520, *Exsurge Domine*, excommunicated Luther.

The war-like rhetoric and behavior of the sixteenth and seventeenth centuries continued. We have dismissed questions of essence, and the battles have sometimes pulled the church's singing into their wake.[6] "A Mighty Fortress" is perhaps the most obvious illustration of a hymn turned into a battle cry,[7] though Luther regarded that hymn as one of comfort. There's a battle in that hymn, but it's not a battle against our neighbors. It's a battle against evil. It's a battle waged and won by God on behalf of the whole world. That means the whole creation, which includes all of us and all of our neighbors—*all* of our neighbors, not just the ones in our country, or in our part of the church, or in our particular tribe, or in any of the ingrown circles we create.

Celebrating the Reformation

So then, what does celebrating the five-hundredth anniversary of the Reformation in 2017—or remembering it in any year—propel us to do? Here are two suggestions. The first is of a general nature, the second relates to the more specific concerns of those who are concerned with hymnody.

1. Tell the truth with honesty and compassion

Much of what has divided Catholics and Protestants is not about central issues, but about a rhetoric of suspicion, hatred, and prejudice. It has been tied to extraneous matters—ones related to the state, to politics, to power struggles, to money, and to attempts to gain control—as much or more than confessional stances. That makes for a confusing mix which is hard to disentangle. But disentangle it we must, because we will not be served well by minimizing or avoiding genuine differences which need to be discussed openly, honestly, and compassionately. And we will not be served well by falsehoods that misrepresent one another and press divisions that are not only superficial or nonexistent, but are downright false, hurtful, and the exact opposite of what God calls us to do.

Fortunately, we have help. John Witvliet, Director of the Calvin Institute of Christian Worship and a professor at Calvin College and Seminary, as well as a prolific writer, editor, and generative source of projects related to the church's music and worship, has provided us with a pastoral approach

---

6. See, for example, Fischer, *Music and Religious Identity in Counter-Reformation Augsburg 1580–1630.*

7. See Cherwien, *"Trutzlied or Trostlied?"* 387–397.

in which he cites Reformed/Catholic studies.[8] In 2013 Lutherans and Catholics produced *From Conflict to Communion.*[9] Two years later, in 2015, relying on fifty years of discussions, the Evangelical Lutheran Church in America, along with the United States Conference of Catholic Bishops, produced *Declaration on the Way: Church, Ministry, and Eucharist.*[10] These are among the joint attempts to forge constructive dialogues. They isolate central issues and longstanding, destructive battles. They help us tell the truth honestly and compassionately in order to forge a constructive path.

2. Live out what hymns express

Telling the truth in the general sense I just described, with the help of these documents, is important and undergirds whatever we may do, whoever we are. At first blush it may not seem to have much to do with hymns or those who are concerned about them. However, the hymnody of the church is more instructive and potent than we may at first think, and its celebration in a particular historical stream helps us see that.

George Black—an astute church musician, professor at Huron College, and President of the Hymn Society in the United States and Canada from 1992 to 1994—once said that the Hymn Society includes people from traditions "you know about and some you may never have heard about." Also, as many of its members know, the Hymn Society is largely made up of people who are not concerned about how to trumpet their particular "thing," but who genuinely seek to learn from one another and from hymnody. The nature of hymns itself generates this perspective among people who are concerned about them. It suggests that we should both celebrate our hymnic heritage and take hold of its power.

Celebrating our hymnic heritage

Since the anniversary of the Reformation uses 1517 as the year when Luther posted the Ninety-Five Theses, the central feature of such a celebration in a hymnic sense centers around the chorale, which Lutherans developed. The chorale is no single isolated thing, however, just like all of our other hymnic strands. The chorale is dependent, at the very least, on Gregorian chant and *Leisen*; it stimulated a huge congregational, choral,

---

8. Witvliet, "Commemorating the Reformation for the 500th Time."

9. The Lutheran World Federation and The Pontifical Council for Promoting Christian Unity, *From Conflict to Communion: Lutheran-Catholic Commemoration of the Reformation in 2017.*

10. Committee for Ecumenical and Interreligious Affairs, United States Conference of Catholic Bishops, Evangelical Lutheran Church in America. .

and organ repertoire; and it has migrated to many parts of the world—like Slovakia, England, the United States, and several countries in Asia and Africa—where it has stimulated continuing hymnic developments and where it has lived side by side with other ones. If you structure a hymn festival around the chorale, therefore, you invariably get something like the hymn festival that Michael Burkhardt[11] structured for the Hymn Society in 2017, when it celebrated the Reformation. You get lament, rejoicing, and thanksgiving centered around German chorales and their settings. At the same time, you are also likely to get what Burkhardt included—hymns and tunes from many places like Scandinavia, Korea, Wales, Slovakia, and from sources like African American spirituals, southern white spirituals, or the Taizé Community in France. Linguistic and musical backgrounds came from Latin and Gregorian chant, as did translations by Gerald Thorson of the United States and Catherine Winkworth of Great Britain. Music and arrangements came from Christoph Weyse, Geonyong Lee, Melchior Vulpius, Martin Luther, Jacques Berthier, Joseph Funk, Dietrich Buxtehude, Felix Mendelssohn, and Burkhardt himself.

The Hymn Society festival was not unique in this rich mix. In February of 2017, I provided the commentary for a hymn festival at Sinai Lutheran Church, a Swedish church in Fremont, Nebraska. Claire Bushong is the organist there. David Schack, who served as organist and choirmaster at First Lutheran Church in Omaha and taught at Concordia University in Seward, played the hymn festival. It was part of a dedication series for a new organ by Juget-Sinclair, celebrating the 125th anniversary of the church and the 500th anniversary of the Reformation. The instrument is a small organ that fits and fills the space extremely well in both sound and sight, but it points to the remarkable breadth of the church's song well beyond its small size or one tradition. All around its case, just above the key desk and below the pipes, the builder has engraved the word "Holy" in twelve languages: Arabic, English, French, German, Greek, Hebrew, Hindi, Italian/Spanish, Latin, Swedish, and Pawnee. This multiplicity of languages points to the breadth of the church's song. So does the choice of the word "Holy." That word is a reference to the central musical event at the weekly communion services at Sinai Church now and throughout the church for the last two millennia.

---

11. Michael Burkhardt is a gifted organist and composer who leads hymn festivals and clinics, works with children, and has authored church music resources and is a graduate of Carthage College, Southern Methodist University, and Arizona State University.

The hymnody of the church points to an undercurrent of breadth, ballast, and health below the surface that, though it is not most visible, nonetheless provides vision for steering the ship on a salutary journey. The church has sometimes lost its vision and found itself in deadly battles and conflicts, especially when it has gotten into bed with the state or allowed the pressures and lures of money to exercise undue control. The Reformation and its aftermath have unfortunately been sucked into these battles, but in the church's hymnody the Reformation points in a much more constructive direction. It points to what will not be confined to our ingrown self-interests and battles with our neighbors, and it leads us to sing with one another no matter where we stand on the spectrum. We need to celebrate that heritage—and to lay hold of its power.

Laying hold of its power

There are two parts to laying hold of its power: the first is about a global view, the second a local one.

- Global -

The song of the church by its very nature has global breadth. Those who care about hymns and help congregations sing them by their very nature study, celebrate, and sing this breadth in what they do regularly, not only at anniversaries and special occasions. We need to affirm and lay hold of that identity again and again—with a continuing, quiet, passionate, and compassionate persistence—for ourselves and for the church and the world around us.

I am not talking here about anything specific that we should or should not do. We can figure out specifics together as we move forward with the checks and balances of our mutual conversations and actions. What I am talking about here is something else, a perspective generated by the church's song. It's a perspective that is not sucked into the state or its priorities, that does not superimpose something from outside itself, and that does not seek easy fixes that mirror our fallen world. It grows instead out of the being and long experience of the church at song. In spite of the horror stories we know about and in spite of the obstacles we face, we live with the same situation that our sisters and brothers have experienced before us. Details change, but the panorama remains the same. Next to all of our bad behavior and the world's systemic disease, there still are, as there always have been, amazingly healthy and constructive oases where pastors, musicians, poets, and assemblies of the church sing and work together. They figure out what to do in the world they are called to serve. This figuring out in part grows out of the church's singing which goes on in spite of conscious or unconscious attempts to destroy it. The singing goes on underneath other battles that may momentarily obscure it, but cannot stop it. It goes on no matter what. As in the Psalms, praise of God always leads to justice and peace. There is deep shalom here, and with it a holistic sense of selfless selfhood and joy in living.

Christopher Page, Professor of Medieval Music and Literature at the University of Cambridge, refers to this shalom by referencing someone we might not expect him to reference in a discussion of the church's singing. It's Tertullian, the stern second-century African theologian. In a discussion of what "necessities of this life remain until, and only until, the life itself be transferred from temporality to eternity,"[12] Tertullian says we have been given "a mouth for eating and drinking: why not rather for speaking [and] praising God?"[13] That is, says Page, the baser functions of the body will pass away, but "vocal praise of God…is one of the principal continuities between the states of bodily life on either side of the grave."[14] Page then says this:

> It is the combination of eschatological hope and diligent domesticity—the desire to stand *sub specie aeternitatis* and yet to walk in the common street as a respected householder with a body not in itself a source of disgrace—that gives the first two centuries of evidence for Christian psalmody their especially moving character.[15]

What Page isolates here is not only evident in the first two centuries. It is evident throughout the history of the church in its singing. It is still evident among us, as in the Hymn Society and in all the constructive oases in the church. Let us continue to lay hold of its reality and power, with persistent boldness on our journey. Or, as Pope Francis said, "Let us sing as we go."[16]

- Local -

What does that mean for us here and now? It becomes clear from a reading of virtually any part of the world's history that the state may do good things. It may support schools and a wide variety of constructive studies including the arts, for example, and it may support justice and peace. But the state cannot be trusted to do those things, and it may do just the

---

12. Tertullian, *Treatise on the Resurrection*, 179.

13. ibid, 181.

14. Page, *The Christian West and Its Singers*, 49.

15. ibid, 50.

16. Francis, *Laudato Si'*, 244.

opposite. Nor can the church, its institutions, or its leaders be trusted, especially when they collapse into the state or its priorities and make the market into God.[17] In our time no reading of history is needed to get this message, though an honest celebration of the Reformation, which includes hymnody, helps us to see it more clearly. It helps us to see that for meaningful life together, with networks for the common good, we have to look below the surface of the evils we face. One place we can look to is our hymnody and the places where communities of healthy song and work are found.

A celebration of our hymnic heritage gives us perspective. The singing of the whole church, by Lutherans and everybody else, in its psalms and hymns, with their inevitable thanksgiving in glory to God, followed by peace and good will toward our neighbors, is part of what has led to the founding of schools, learning, study, disciplines, curiosity, the search for truth, hospitals, other houses of care, and systems that seek the common good.[18] It is no accident that we find the following examples:

- Ambrose, the "father of the church's song," as the bishop of Milan in the fourth century, championed the cause of the poor and the oppressed.

- Guido d'Arezzo, three years after he demonstrated staff notation in 1028, opposed the buying of ecclesiastical offices.

- Johann Crüger, the cantor whose *Praxis Pietatis Melica* was the most important seventeenth-century Lutheran hymnal, attempted to bring a plan to the electoral court to end the Thirty Years' War.[19]

- At the center of Martin Schalling's hymn "Lord, Thee I Love with All My Heart," the last stanza of which J. S. Bach used to conclude his setting of the *St. John Passion*, there are these lines: "Lord, grant that I in every place may glorify thy lavish grace and serve and help my neighbor."[20]

---

17. See Cox, *The Market as God*, and comments related to this book by Stephanie Paulsell, "When the Market is God," as well as a book review by Philip Hefner. See also: Tornielli and Galeazzi, *This Economy Kills*.

18. For a similar list, see Chapter 20.

19. Howard, "Johann Crüger as a Music Theorist," 6.

20. The hymn in Catherine Winkworth's altered English translation can be found in *Evangelical Lutheran Worship*, #750.

- The hymnologist and hymnal editor Percy Dearmer championed social justice and opened a canteen for the unemployed at Westminster Abbey when he became a canon there in 1931.
- Jeffrey Rowthorn and Russell Schulz-Widmar in 2014 compiled *Sing of a World Made New: Hymns of Justice, Peace and Christian Responsibility.*

If we look at five hundred years of congregational song since the Reformation, it should not go unnoticed, as Chad Fothergill points out, "that cantors of the sixteenth, seventeenth, and eighteenth centuries were involved in an array of disciplines beyond music, including law, philosophy, mathematics, medicine, literature, and poetry—a panoply reflective of their humanist training in classical liberal arts subjects through the Protestant educational model established by Luther and Melanchthon"[21] which built on the work Page recounts in the first ten centuries of the church's history. Nor should we miss the schools that were founded, where these musicians and their fellow citizens studied, nor the singing and the breadth of learning that was fostered in them.

Remembering these things is not an exercise in nostalgia. A lot of hand-wringing characterizes our life at the moment. That is largely because, by getting stuck in our local contexts and by making up a nostalgic past, we collapse everything into the state, its control, institutions, data, perspective, and the importance of the world's power and money as if they were God. We forget what the twelfth-century monk Bernard of Cluny taught us: "The world is very evil."[22] And, as Emily Brink, a past President of the Hymn Society, said to me when I made a comment about money in these connections, "This is not about money, Paul. It's about vision."

The panoply of study that Chad Fothergill reminds us about is related to the vision that Emily Brink wisely reminded me about, which is in turn related to the vision implicit in hymnody's subversively constructive undercurrent.[23] We might remember another twelfth-century monk, Bernard of

---

21. Fothergill is an organist who, at the time of this writing, is completing his doctoral degree in the Boyer College of Music and Dance at Temple University in Philadelphia, where he is studying the Lutheran cantorial tradition. "Doctor, Lawyer, Poet, Mayor…and Cantor? Early Lutheran Church Musicians and Vocation," 15.

22. Neale, *Collected Hymns, Sequences, and Carols,* 203.

23. This undercurrent is confirmed in an article about the singing of the *Agnus Dei* at the breaking of the bread in the Eucharist and its association with justice and martyrdom. See Busted, "AGNUS DEI: The Cost of Discipleship," 41–42.

Clairvaux, who said that "hearing will restore your vision."[24] We might gloss his comment to say that "hymn-singing will restore your vision," which may be part of what he had in mind. Proverbs 29:18 reminds us that without vision the people perish. Our hymnody helps to provide vision. We are not dependent on the state, institutions we create, or dollars and their power. Dollars, like everything else in our world, are included in our vision, of course. But our vision is the base of concern for everybody, which paradoxically includes the state, even when it does not support us. Vision leads us wherever we need to go—which is not only, or even primarily, to a concern for dollars and their power.

The vision the church's hymnody gives us is imbedded in the worship where hymns were sung. It begins in the sounds of glory to God and leads to our vocations in God's creation. "Glory to God" has characterized the singing at the beginning of much of the church's weekly worship, including what we celebrate from the last five hundred years and still sing today. Following "glory to God" we remember God's gracious mercy for us, and we confess our ingratitude and the mess that ingratitude lands us in. Then, at the end of the service, we sing "grant us peace," and we hear God's call to go in peace and serve our neighbors.

That call is not specific to now, nor has it ever been specific. It means that we are to sing of a world made new, singing as we go and figuring out what justice and peace require of us where we live and work. Examples from our past can inspire us in our time and place to construct the schools and the study, the service and the care, the techniques and the skills, and the networks of concern for the other. Those who came before us through their versions of these things have made possible what we have received as gifts, which in turn have helped us to sing what we are called to sing and to do what we are called to do.

The work we have to do, as the work our forebears had to do, is complex and difficult. It is not easy to do, let alone figure out, because it includes the perplexities of our age, the disciplines of hymnody, all of the study they presume, concerns for others individually, and the communal networks of influence and power that seek peace and justice for the whole world.

Fortunately, we have help, not only from the past, but from the present. An example is the Hymn Society's recent collection of hymns called *Singing Welcome: Hymns and Songs of Hospitality to Refugees and Immigrants*. Another example is the regular meetings of the Association of Lutheran

---

24. Lawlor, "Geometry in the Service of Prayer: Reflections on Cistercian Mystic Architecture," 16.

Church Musicians (ALCM), and in particular the Minneapolis meeting in 2017. Mary Louise Bringle, a Presbyterian hymn writer, perceptively analyzed for the ALCM what she calls the "identity-relevance dilemma," with insights to help light our way. A little later on the same day, Anthony Ruff, a church musician and church music scholar, welcomed Lutherans to St. John's Abbey in Collegeville, Minnesota, for evening prayer, where Catholic monks and Lutherans together remembered the five-hundredth anniversary of the Reformation.

The work may not be easy, but we have help from the past and the present. Paradoxically, the burden is light, and the duty is delight. We can do this, not in some great public display or misguided simplistic solution by which we presume to solve all of our problems or save the world, but in our daily vocations as poets, pastors, musicians, or whatever, wherever they lead us. Leave the hand-wringing behind. Celebrate our hymnic heritage. Lay hold of its power. Like those who came before us, we can figure this out, day by day, on behalf of the dysfunctional culture that surrounds us, for the glory of God and for the good of our neighbors.

Let us sing as we go.

＃

18

J. S. Bach and the Clavierübung

Clavierübung III

In the Fall/Winter 2014 issue of *CrossAccent*, the journal of the Association of Lutheran Church Musicians, Chad Fothergill discussed connections to funerals in Bach's E-Flat Major Fugue, BWV 552,[1] the piece at the end of the third volume of the *Clavierübung*. Those connections help us understand the *Clavierübung* as a whole and especially the third volume, and they helped me begin to answer some questions that have repeatedly puzzled me about this collection of organ pieces.

The *Clavierübung* ("Keyboard Practice") contains in its subtitle, "for music lovers to refresh their spirits," which Christoph Wolff, a musicologist and authority on Bach, views as a summary of Bach's vocation. He says, "For Bach the ultimate rationale for being a musician, that is, a performer-composer, was not to pursue some sort of mental construct, but 'to make a well-sounding harmony to the honor of God and the permissible delectation of the soul.'"[2] The *Clavierübung* is a set of four volumes, the first with six partitas, the second with the *Italian Concerto* and *French Overture*, the third discussed below, and the fourth the *Goldberg Variations*. The four parts of this set are, to quote Wolff again, "a systematic and complete survey of the art of keyboard music as seen from Bach's perspective."[3]

---

1. Fothergill, "Bach's Benediction: The E-Flat Major Fugue, BWV 552, and the Christian Funeral Liturgy," 23–29.

2. Wolff, *Johann Sebastian Bach: The Learned Musician*, 308–309. Wolff is quoting Bach. See David and Mendel, *The New Bach Reader*, 16-17, though the last word in *The New Bach Reader* is "spirit," not "soul."

3. Wolff, *Johann Sebastian Bach*, 375.

The third volume of the *Clavierübung* consists of the following:

- The E-Flat Major Prelude
- Settings of chorales which are metrical versions of the first two parts of the Ordinary of the Mass—the Kyrie and the Gloria
- Settings of chorales related to the Catechism
- Four duets
- The E-Flat Major Fugue

As is often noted, Trinitarian threes are everywhere. There are three flats in both the Prelude and Fugue, three related ideas in the Prelude, and three subjects in the Fugue. There are two sets of three settings of the Kyrie (6 divisible by 3), three settings of the Gloria, and two settings for each of the six Catechism chorales (a total of 12 which is divisible by 3). The total number of chorale settings is 21 (divisible by 3), and the four duets plus the Prelude and Fugue bring the overall total to 27 pieces (divisible by 3). It seems clear that the presence of all of these threes grounds the volume in a Trinitarian conception. Is there anything beyond that?

The third volume of the *Clavierübung* has been called an "Organ Mass" or the "Catechism Chorales." If the former, it is a *Missa Brevis*, since only the first two of the five parts of the Ordinary are present. But then, why are the Catechism chorales there? If it is the Catechism chorales, why are the chorales from the Ordinary there? And why are the four duets there at all? Malcolm Boyd, in his commentary on Bach, refers to their presence as "enigmatic."[4] Albert Schweitzer, another Bach expert, says they were "accidentally included during the engraving."[5] This has long perplexed me, so I set out to analyze the duets to see what I could find.

The Four Duets

David Jenkins, Liturgical Music Director at St. Paul Seminary in Minneapolis, played an organ recital where he remarked that the duets are "two-part inventions on caffeine." Indeed, they pull into play all sorts of dense and skillful contrapuntal writing. That is not surprising for Bach, but are the duets only included for their compositional skill? If so, why are the other pieces there? Bach could have written a whole book of pieces like the duets if he wanted a volume about compositional skill.

4. Boyd, *Bach*, 195.

5. Schweitzer, *J. S. Bach*, 289.

Then I noticed that subtle thematic hints in the duets relate to the settings of the chorale that precedes them and to the E-Flat Major Fugue that follows.

- The scale in the first duet turns the scale in the first setting of the chorale "Jesus Christus, unser Heiland" upside down and extends it, pointing forward to the scale in the tail of the coming first fugue subject.

- The leaps in the left hand of the first duet are derived from the leaps in the first setting of the same chorale.

- The fugue subject of the second duet fills out the triad implied in the subject of the second setting of the chorale.

- The left hand of the third duet begins the way the beginning of the third fugue subject begins.

- The subject of the fourth duet points to the coming first fugue subject in an inverted form.

These hints suggested that it might be wise to look at the preceding chorales that Bach chose to set and especially at the last one, "Jesus Christus, unser Heiland."

The six chorales that Bach set after the Kyrie and the Gloria were written by Martin Luther for the six parts of the Catechism: the Ten Commandments, the Nicene Creed, the Lord's Prayer, Baptism, Confession of Sins, and the Eucharist. The last of these, the one for the Eucharist, "Jesus Christus, unser Heiland," as Schweitzer notes, is out of place since Confession, not the Eucharist, is the last topic in the Catechism. Schweitzer thought that "it is impossible to say why" Bach made this placement which is "not correct."[6] Maybe it is possible to say why, and maybe Bach knew what he was doing and why he did it. He knew the order of the Catechism and could have followed it rather than the order he chose.

"Jesus Christus, unser Heiland" for the Eucharist is based on a Latin hymn; in the process of revising it, Luther cast it into German. Here is his tenth and last stanza:

> *Die Frucht soll auch nicht ausblieben,*
> *Deinen Nächsten sollst du lieben.*
> *Dass er dein geniessen kann,*
> *Wie dein Gott in dir getan.*[7]

---

6. Schweitzer, *J. S. Bach*, 290.

7. Aufdemberge, *Christian Worship: Handbook*, 338.

Here is an English translation:

> *Let this food your faith so nourish*
> *That its fruit of love may flourish*
> *And your neighbor learn from you*
> *How much God's wondrous love can do.*[8]

This chorale that relates to the Eucharist and directly precedes the duets is then about being nourished by Christ's body and blood, and being sent into the world to love our neighbors as Christ's body with the fruits of the gifts God gives us. Perhaps Bach placed it where he did because it leads to sending us on our vocations from the church's worship, and Bach wanted to build that sequence into the collection called the *Clavierübung*. Perhaps the duets were not accidentally included in the *Clavierübung III*, but were quite purposefully placed by Bach exactly where they are.

Sending and Vocation

While puzzling over the *Clavierübung III*, I was also working on an assignment from the Worship Dialogue in Minneapolis to speak about the sending at the end of the Mass. Assembling information about this topic in the church's worship from Justin Martyr—a second-century Christian apologist who gives us insights into the church's worship—to the present made it clear that, though the historic dismissal formulas and actions lack specificity, they play off of the peace in the third petition of the Agnus Dei ("Grant us peace") that is sung at communion, and they often employ words like the ones we still use, "Go in peace; serve the Lord." It also became clear that the peace at the Agnus Dei does not come out of nowhere, but is present at the beginning of the Mass in the Gloria ("peace to God's people on earth") and during the service at the kiss of peace ("Peace be with you"). A trajectory of the peace Christ brings is present in Word and Sacrament throughout weekly worship and then is extended to the whole world as Christians leave worship and carry it out as Christ's body throughout the week in their various vocations. Worship leads the church into the world. The lack of specificity in the sending rite means each person, in his or her vocation, individually and communally, has to figure out what it means to go in Christ's peace. Is it doing the best possible craft of his or her vocation, is it giving a cup of cold water to a neighbor, is it suggested by the parable of the Good Samaritan in whatever circumstances that may bring, is it a

---

8. *Lutheran Service Book*, #627.

more systemic move of organizing or participating in a march for peace and justice, or is it being a good parent? For each individual, is it all of these things, more or less, or something different?

Bach and the *Clavierübung III*

I began to realize that the sending from worship was related to Luther's deep concern about vocation.[9] I was aware that Bach knew not only about that, but also about other themes of the church catholic that Luther and the Lutheran stream have embraced and embodied. I began to sense that maybe Bach was getting at something profound by characteristically hiding it and revealing it in his music. Maybe the duets had something to do with taking up the vocation on which the Christian is sent. So, I did something I once considered crazy and a complete waste of time, until some years ago, when I kept accidentally stumbling over it and finally could not deny it any more: I started counting.

The relationship of music to proportions and numbers, including numeric symbolism in music generally and in Bach's music particularly, is a disputed and complicated topic. Early in my life I was quite skeptical about it. I remain skeptical when it seems stretched to unduly imaginative lengths. But as I kept finding it—mostly by accident—in Bach's scores, I was forced to conclude that its presence is undeniable. He did not invent it. It is present in his time and long before that into ancient understandings. He simply employed it—quite creatively.

Numeric symbolism is not only found in music. Take "O MorningStar, How Fair and Bright" (*WIE SCHÖN LEUCHTET DER MORGENSTERN*) which we call the "Queen of the Chorales." With this work, sixteenth-century composer Philipp Nicolai created a hymn that looks like a chalice when you lay it out poetically. In that connection, he emphasized this line: "Dein Wort, dein Geist, dein Leib und Blut." An English translation that can be sung to the same tune reads, "Your word and Spirit, flesh and blood." He accomplished this emphasis by putting that line at the very center of the hymn as a turning point. The center here means not only what we might consciously or unconsciously realize in a general way as we look at or sing the hymn. It means precisely at the very middle of the middle stanza of seven stanzas,

---

9. See, for example, Wingren, *Luther on Vocation*. For a discussion that grows out of a Lutheran perspective and has a chapter on Luther, see Heiges, *The Christian's Calling*. For a broad ecumenical overview, also with chapters on Luther, see Placher, ed., *Callings: Twenty Centuries of Christian Wisdom on Vocation*.

with exactly twenty-one words before it and twenty-one words after it. Twenty-one is seven, the perfect number, times three, the Trinity.

It is hard to see how that could have been accidental, or how the numbers one finds in Bach's scores are accidental. They cannot be heard and do not improve or worsen the music. Bach's music stands on its own in sound. Numeric symbolism nevertheless does indicate the thought that went into the composing. If these numbers confirm what the music itself is doing, one gets deeper insights into Bach's intentions.[10] It should be added that, contrary to how numbers have been used for nefarious or occult purposes, Christians, and particularly Bach, have used them in a very different way, namely, to serve the radical freedom and life offered by the gospel.

I discovered that the number of measures in the four duets are 73, 149, 39, and 108, and that if you add those together you get 369. 369 divided by 9, which is three 3s, equals 41. The threes point again to the Trinity, but now we also have 41, which, as is widely known, is the sum of the letters of Bach's name.[11] Bach appears to be running out his vocation as a musician and composer with the finest craft and giving us all an example for our various vocations, whatever they happen to be. Peter Williams, an organist and musicologist, notes the craft that they involved.

> The four duets in...*Clavierübung III* systematically include maximum varieties of pulse, meter, time-signature, mode, key, form, imitation, counterpoint, motif, chromaticism and diatonicism, as if each of these were a pre-planned item to be ticked off on a 'list of things to do'. In being so systematic, the Duets are 'tidying up' the looser kind of counterpoint usually found in duos elsewhere, especially those in French organ masses.[12]

Then I noticed something else in the overall construction of the *Clavierübung III*. The key centers of the last four chorale settings for the Kyrie and the Gloria match the keys of the four duets.[13] Could it be that Bach is telling us that worship drives us to our various crafts throughout the Christian life, a life which is summarized by the themes of the Catechism

---

10. For summaries of this topic, with wise cautions, see Geck, "Proportion and Numerical Relations in Bach's Music," *Johann Sebastian Bach: Life and Work*, 670–674, and, with mention of the *Clavierübung*, Williams, *Bach: A Musical Biography*, 563–566.

11. J-S-B-A-C-H (J=9 [I and J are interchangeable], S=18, B=2, A=1, C=3, H=8).

12. Williams, *Bach: A Musical Biography*, 363.

13. E minor, F, G, and A major in the chorale settings and E minor, F and G major, and A minor in the duets.

and which plays off the peace in the Agnus Dei and the sending into the world? Does the Prelude at the beginning of the *Clavierübung III*, and the Fugue, with its funeral connections at the end, point to the whole trajectory of the Christian life, from birth to death, all grounded in the communal perichoretic music and welcome of the Trinity? The theologian Robert Jenson aptly summarizes this Trinitarian welcome in this sentence: "God is a great fugue, and there is nothing so capacious as a fugue."[14]

Checks

Is this a crazy idea, analysis gone wild, numeric symbolism unduly stretched? Maybe, but maybe not. Checks in a couple other pieces by Bach suggest it's not so crazy.

My cantor Gary Butler at the Lutheran Church of the Resurrection in Roseville, Minnesota, deploys me to prepare and conduct a Bach cantata on one Sunday each year at the regular Sunday Eucharist. The cantata is sung in the service of the Word just as it was intended and used in Bach's Leipzig. While I was trying to figure out the *Clavierübung III* and the assignment from Worship Dialogue, I was therefore also studying the score of Bach's Cantata No. 129, *Gelobet sei der Herr* ("All Praise to God the Lord") which we were doing that year. We had done this cantata at the church some years earlier, so I revisited my notes and remembered that I had unexpectedly stumbled on the following and had written it up like this for a forum.

> Cantata 129 is a paean of praise to the Trinity. The first three stanzas of the hymn praise God as the Creator, Redeemer, and Sustainer. The fourth stanza praises God as the Three in One. These four lead to the last stanza where we join the choirs of saints and angels in a jubilant "Holy, Holy, Holy."
>
> Behind this musical celebration of the Trinity, Bach hides a perceptive insight. He links the first and last choruses by 3 long—Trinitarian—trumpet notes, 2 in the first chorus, 1 in the last. Each of the first 2 long notes ends with 5 more notes, making 6 times 2, or 12. Only one note is added to the third long note, adding 2 more and making 14 notes for all 3 together. 14 is the numerical value of B-A-C-H. The 3 long notes are audible just as the baptismal actions with water in the name of the Father, Son, and Holy Spirit are visible. The 14 notes are more hidden.

---

14. Jenson, *Systematic Theology, Volume 1, The Triune God*, 236.

What is completely hidden, however, is this: the first chorus has 90 measures, the last chorus 33. 90 plus 33 is 123 which, when divided by the Trinitarian number 3, equals 41. 41, the reverse of 14, is the numerical value of J-S-B-A-C-H. Bach, by pointing to his baptism, signals all of our baptisms and where baptism leads us—to the hidden acts of our various vocations under God's call and blessing.

And then there's this. In his Mass in B Minor, which is both a musical and a theological testament, Bach uses the same music for the *Gratias agimus tibi propter magnum gloria tuum* ("We give you thanks for your great glory") of the Gloria and for the Dona nobis pacem ("Grant us peace") of the Agnus Dei. The doxology near the beginning leads to peace at the end of the final movement. The doxology of worship leads to the peace Christ gives, which Christians, as Christ's body, are called to carry into the world in their vocations.

I unexpectedly received another insight at a colloquium on church music and the Reformation at the end of September in 2017 at Baylor University. David Music, a distinguished hymnologist and professor at Baylor, had asked me to give the opening and closing lectures at the colloquium. Seven papers had been chosen from a group of submissions, and in between some of those papers the schedule included a session on Singing and Playing of Reformation Hymns. When I arrived, I discovered that *Clavierübung III* provided the hymns that were to be used. Interesting and perceptive choice, I thought. It was more perceptive and helpful than I initially thought and confirmed what I've found in *Clavierübung III*.

We sang the six Catechism hymns, after which we heard a setting of each one from *Clavierübung III*. Isabelle Demers, a marvelous organist and professor of organ at Baylor, along with her students, played the settings. She played the first of the two settings that precedes the duets and is related to the Eucharist, "Jesus Christus, unser Heiland." This is a trio. A widely leaping figure begins with eighth notes, is joined in the seventh measure by rapidly moving cascades of sixteenth notes, under which the pedal enters at measure eighteen with the hymn tune in long dotted half notes. The listener hears a jubilant swirl of forward motion.

Sam Eatherton, one of Isabelle Demers' students who played, wrote the program notes which said that the initial widely leaping figure is a "cross motive" which points to "the centrality of Christ as present in the sacrament for the strengthening of faith," and pointed out that this figure occurs 72 times. I asked Isabelle Demers what 72 signifies, but she didn't know.

From my earlier research, I didn't believe that 72 was a coincidence, and eventually realized that 72 is the number of disciples sent out by Jesus in Luke 10:1 to bring peace to their neighbors. It seems that Bach coupled the presence of Christ in the Eucharist to our going out—leaping—with joy to bring Christ's peace to our neighbors, followed by the duets which exemplify Bach's vocation with the implication that we are each to figure out on our own.

Further insights came in November of 2017 from three faculty members at Eastman School of Music where I discussed this topic as part of a lecture at the Utech Hymnody Symposium. David Higgs and Dan Zager pointed me to Ruth Tatlow's copious study of numbers in Bach,[15] and William Porter to Albert Clement's discussion of the four Duets.[16] Tatlow's detail about the way Bach added and revised the duets indicates careful intent on multiple levels of meaning. Clement suggests that Bach had home use in mind for the four duets and that they represent the "four sweet things" of Heinrich Müller's "Von vier süssen Dingen" in his *Haus- und Tisch-Andachten* (*House- and Table-Devotions*) from 1666. These four things—the Word of God, the cross, not fearing death, and yearning for heaven—permeate a Christian's vocation in the world. None of this addresses what I have found, but it supports and harmonizes with it. Robin Leaver's comments about the duets in relation to the daily life of prayer and practice, plus the overall sweep of his thoughts, suggest more explicit support.[17]

Clavierübung III may indeed be about the Christian life—pointing to Bach's musical vocation as composer-performer in the church's worship and beyond it, with the duets a symbol for the other volumes. In the process, Bach points to the vocations of other Christians, whoever they may be and whatever they may do.

---

15. Ruth Tatlow, *Bach's Numbers*, especially 182–190.

16. Albert Clement, "A Case of Liturgical Practice in Johann Sebastian Bach's Home."

17. See Robin Leaver, "Bach's 'Clavierübung III': Some Historical and Theological Considerations," especially 28–30.

19

Paul Manz:
Music in the Service of the Gospel

First Hearing Paul Manz Play

I do not remember when I first heard Paul Manz play. It was before his now well-known reputation as Cantor at Mount Olive Lutheran Church in Minneapolis and a skilled improviser and leader of hymn festivals. It may have been at a chapel service during the summer of 1966 at the Schola Cantorum at Concordia Seminary in St. Louis. I do remember what I immediately thought. It was the same thing I always have thought when hearing a fine musician: "Westermeyer, why are you in this business at all?" I had learned by then, however, and have continued to learn what I have also told my students: "It's not your job to be Paul Manz. It's your job to be who you are and to use whatever talents you have as well as possible. You can learn from Paul Manz. Now, knock it off, and get going."

So, that first impression quickly evaporated, but the one that came at virtually the same time did not go away. It was this: "What is he doing? This is not business as usual. So what's going on here?"

Business as Usual

The training of pastors and church musicians among us generally happens in two tracks. Pastors are trained in seminaries or programs of theological study, and musicians are trained in conservatories or programs of musical study. The two tracks usually do not intersect. There are exceptions where fruitful exchanges and sharing happen, and there are individuals who work at the intersections. But most of us are part of a system with two mutually exclusive tracks. Musically, however, they both live in the shadow of the nineteenth century. When the nineteenth century calls the shots, music is perceived to be what trained professional or semi-professional artists do as popular or classical performers, either by themselves alone or in ensembles of various kinds—or, in our period, with recordings. This is out of reach for most people, so they only listen to what the virtuosos serve up. That is a fine and worthy situation until it becomes the only thing and obscures or shuts down everything else. Church choirs and church organists—and certainly singing congregations—are, at best, second-class citizens in this system, unless they are among the few virtuosos who perform music at the highest professional level. Both pastors and musicians share the same presupposition here, that music is about technical skill. That is what justifies it.

This system, especially with recordings, sets up music as the production of artifacts of high quality, however that quality is defined. Musicians are primed to look down on what happens musically in the church, just as pastors are primed to call musicians out-of-touch elitists. That produces separate sets of evaluative judgments. The practical result is control by power plays, or, in an attempt to avoid those, acceptance of any music in any condition. In short, the divide between theology and music creates what Erik Routley already half a century ago called "at best...patronage from church to music" together with "tentative moralisms from musicians to musicians."[1]

Pastors and musicians of course know that music is more than notes and their proper execution. Most pastors and musicians know very well that music cannot be reduced to technique. Music's relationships to devotion, contemplation, and emotion with religious or quasi-religious themes have been embedded in our culture since the eighteenth century[2] and well before that. There is an inner necessity and the historical push of inertia for the church to sing and use music, but in the absence of theological reflection or knowledge that any such reflection even exists, there is no way to determine what music fits or doesn't fit the church's worship or why music is there at all. Because of this, music gravitates to technical facility and then to the culture's tendency to use that facility in the service of selling things, all in the context of a general religious or quasi-religious musical haze. It would be as if pastoral care were omitted from seminary curricula and the church's wisdom about it remained inaccessible except to the few who sought to study it on their own.

---

1. Routley, *Church Music and Theology*, 110.

2. Anttila, *Luther's Theology of Music*, 1.

It was clear to me that Paul Manz represented a high level of technical skill and performance practice, but the justification for, as well as the context and content of what he was doing, did not fit the system of business as usual. So what was going on? What was he doing? I think the answer is that Manz is one of the clearest representatives of what church musicians are called to do—to use God's gift of music with humility and gratitude in the service of the gospel. Here are some reflections about that.

Music in the Service of the Gospel

I. The New Song

For Paul Manz, music in worship was an event where the new song was being sung. Technical skill, music worth doing, and music worth doing well were very important, but he was not engaged in a performance where music was a pre-packaged item from the past or the present, justified by virtuosic technique and perfection, like a recording with all of the mistakes edited out. Such a recording is to be celebrated and has an important place as study material, high-level recreation and pleasure, a technological exercise, or something like that; but neither it nor any performance of music as a perfect artifact is church music. Music in the service of the gospel is always a lively new song, sung and played in the flesh, here and now, by the actual human beings who are present, with all of the contingencies that brings with it.

The new song which the Psalms summon us to sing is not the culture's definition of what was written yesterday or today. It is rather the new song in Christ, the living voice of the gospel in the moment. This joins the new creation of the church in Christ—the group that is singing—to God's gift of music, which is new every time it is a live phenomenon. The music may have been written centuries ago or yesterday, but it will never before have been sounded as it is sounded in this time and place, because this particular time and place never existed before, and because music's character is to pass through time and be gone. The song of the church is always new in this musical sense and always new in Christ in a theological sense.

Paul Manz understood this, and so he improvised as has been common among church musicians for centuries. But, as for church musicians before him who understood their craft, this improvisation was not a murky glue of meaningless sounds. It was the finest craft, carefully disciplined by the church's message, history, and wisdom, by Manz's own practice, and then lived in the moment. It broke out in the freedom and high adventure disciplined craft makes possible.

When I was writing a biographical sketch of Walter Buszin— a twentieth-century teacher, church musician, editor, musicologist, liturgiologist, and leader in the recovery of the Lutheran liturgical and musical heritage—I discovered that Manz had written Buszin a letter of appreciation when Buszin retired. He said to him, "As an undergraduate student…I heard your lone voice…speaking out in behalf of the goodly musical heritage which is ours."[3] That goodly musical heritage taught Manz. Like Jan Bender—the church organist and composer from the Netherlands who was arrested by the Nazis and who taught in this country at Valparaiso, the University of Denver, Concordia College (Seward), Wittenberg, Concordia Seminary (St. Louis), Gustavus Adolphus, and Southern Seminary—Manz saw music as rooted in the past, but growing and developing in the present.

For Manz, the present meant applying all that the goodly heritage taught in an attentive appreciation for the moment, for what was being sung, for those singing now with his help, using his skills and his ears. Improvisation probably points most obviously to that whole mix, but the specificity of improvisation is not the issue here. The issue is the perspective that drives what the church musician does. Manz improvised, but he also played the church's musical literature.

In his dedicatory recital of the organ at Mount Olive, Manz played a wide swath of literature from across the church's history. He did this with the sense that Yuko Maruyama, one of Luther Seminary's Master of Sacred Music graduates, expressed to me recently in an apt image which makes the point very well. She said, "When I practice hymns for the service, I feel that I am opening a new jar, like strawberry or blueberry jam. Even if I had played the same hymn thousands of times, I always feel that I am practicing the hymn for the first time, just like opening a new jar." Manz was always opening a new jar with the new song, whether improvised by him or with the written music the church has deemed worth keeping—of which there is a wealth, as he knew.

II. Perspective

The issue here is the perspective that drives what the church musician does. If you listened to Manz play, lead a congregation, and direct a choir, you realized pretty quickly that he was not engaged in the culture's musical

---

3. Koriath, *Music for the Church: The Life and Work of Walter E. Buszin*, 16.

business as usual. Even if you could not articulate what was going on and did not know about the new song, you knew that something was different here, something associated with the life and witness of the church. If you happened to come across the foreword Manz wrote for Joy Lawrence's and John Ferguson's *A Musician's Guide to Church Music*, you would have discovered that Manz had in fact thought this out.[4] He did not pretend to be a theologian. That was not his vocation, the same as the theologian's vocation is not that of the musician. But, as a church musician, he was in touch with the church's theology, as theologians are called to be in touch with the church's music. Manz held up the musical part of this "fruitful partnership" in the body of Christ, "bound together" with "penitent gratitude" in its "common humanity" and "glorifying God," to which Erik Routley pointed so well.[5]

Manz explained what church musicians are called to do—something which he understood as complementary to what the ordained clergy are called to do. Like the clergy, he said, musicians "preach...teach...comfort the bereaved and help sustain the weak...counsel the troubled...and...assist at the distribution of the sacrament." They do this, however, not from the pulpit and altar, but from the "choir loft or the organ bench." They "communicate the Word...in a largely nonverbal manner," and the "spiritual"—the *geist*—which is present here "involves each individually and all corporately as the hearts of people pray, praise and give thanks." Manz made clear that "it is precisely this concept of church music that welcomes musicians into the service of the church." And then he explained "this concept" in connection with what it is not. "It is one thing," he said, "to dispense carefully prepared music to the church; it is quite another to offer carefully prepared church music! The difference lies not only in the appropriateness but in the basis for all church art, namely, the *Word*,[6] which he knew is the Living Incarnate Word that transcends all of our words.

There is a lot packed into those brief comments. Manz did not get this concept of and perspective on the church's music out of nowhere. In typical Lutheran fashion, he derived it from the goodly heritage of the church catholic through a Lutheran lens and the accumulated wisdom this heritage gives us. Some explanation about the goodly heritage is in order.

---

4. Lawrence and Ferguson, *A Musician's Guide to Church Music*, vii–viii.

5. Routley, *Church Music and Theology*, 110.

6. The quotations here are from and summarize the three paragraphs that make up Manz's foreword to Lawrence and Ferguson, as cited above.

III. The Goodly Heritage

Not all of the sixteenth-century reformers responded like Luther to the musical heritage of the church which I explained in Chapter 17. Ulrich Zwingli and Zwinglians obliterated this heritage. John Calvin and Calvinists restricted it to unison congregational metrical psalmody and the Word and Table sequence of the Mass, but not the Mass itself. Martin Luther and Lutherans took the whole body of work, ran with it, and developed it further in both its congregational and choral genres, with cleaned-up Latin and German vernacular versions of the Mass. Lutherans expanded the already huge musical repertoire the church had by adding and continuing generation after generation to add more hymns, more hymn tunes, more choral music, more organ music, and more extensive thought about music in the life of the church. That included Luther's admonition to "take special care to shun perverted minds who prostitute this lovely gift of nature and art with their erotic rantings."[7]

Much, probably most of the music from both before and after the sixteenth-century Reformation, from Lutherans and everyone else, has had little staying power beyond its time and place. The church has learned from it, however, and has kept what has borne repetition. This whole mix of what is worth keeping and what is not is the goodly heritage that the whole church and its musicians receive right to the present moment.

In addition to countless anonymous poets and musicians, this heritage in its Lutheran version comes through people like Philipp Nicolai who, following Luther's example, wrote both hymns and their tunes; through those who wrote hymns like Gerhardt, Franzmann, and Vajda; and through those whose vocation was a musical one, like Schütz, Crüger, Bach, Mendelssohn, and Distler. This is the heritage Paul Manz, like Martin Luther, received and learned from. Neither Martin Luther nor Paul Manz were lone rangers. They were servants of the church, wise enough to know that the goodly heritage was a solid foundation on which they could build and from whose mistakes and successes they could learn. It helped to propel them in continuing faithful service to the church and to the world they were called to serve.

IV. The Lutheran Contribution

The goodly heritage of music has many facets, related to the many ways the church catholic has regarded its song. These include music's connection

---

7. Luther, "Preface to Georg Rhau's *Symphoniae iucundae*," 324. For context see Westermeyer, *Te Deum: The Church and Music*, 145.

with praise and thanksgiving, with prayer, with the story of God's faithful mercy, and with the proclamation of the Word. The church, when it sings, cannot avoid and has not avoided any of these facets, but different parts of the church have emphasized different ones. For example, Roman Catholics and Calvinists can be understood to emphasize prayer. Methodists can be understood to emphasize the story. Lutherans have characteristically emphasized the proclamation of the Word—though prayer, praise, and thanksgiving are present also.[8] On October 2, 2016, John Schwandt[9] played an organ recital at Mount Olive Lutheran Church, which duplicated the dedicatory organ recital Paul Manz played there fifty years earlier on October 2, 1966. It is no accident that the recital pointed to the Word and its grace as the "basis for all church art."[10]

There are many complicated theological issues that attend music's relationship to the Word, as Miikka Anttila explains in *Luther's Theology of Music*.[11] It was not Manz's job to unpack them; that is the theologian's task. That he was aware of this theological undergirding and that it infused his vocation is what needs to be understood. And that he was responsible to his particular tradition within the whole church catholic needs to be emphasized—as well as his realization that his particular tradition and its emphasis was part of a larger catholic whole which includes prayer, praise, and thanksgiving with all the saints.

The church's larger catholic whole, in relation to music to which Manz attended, might be summarized by the following: The church has characteristically been organized in local assemblies and groups of these assemblies. In our period we call these congregations and denominations. There is always a temptation to make closed cliques out of these clusters and to pit them against one another in battles. Closed cliques are the antithesis of the church. Differences are important. We learn from them, and they need to be explored and discussed, but using them in ingrown ways as weapons does not square with the Commandments or Jesus' summary of them. And, in fact, the various communities actually serve to highlight different aspects of the Christian faith, such as how music is regarded and pursued. Understanding the various traditions and their work as gifts to the whole

---

8. Anttila, *Luther's Theology of Music*, 100–101.

9. John Schwandt is Associate Professor of Organ and Director of the American Organ Institute at the University of Oklahoma School of Music, a skillful church organist and improviser.

10. Lawrence and Ferguson, *A Musician's Guide to Church Music*, viii.

11. Anttila, *Luther's Theology of Music*, 9–12.

church catholic and world is not only for our good and the good of the neighbor. It also points us to the mosaic that these various traditions form, since our finitude makes it impossible for any one community to embody the whole. Musicians have probably realized both denominational and ecumenical issues more than any other group in the church. This is not because they are better or worse than anybody else. It is because, if they are faithful to their vocation, they encounter the rich tapestry that church music inevitably brings with it. Paul Manz was faithful to his vocation.

The Lutheran musical contribution to the whole centers around the Word and its proclamation. That has infused Lutheran congregational and choral singing, the organ's playing, and the whole proclamatory progression of biblical readings with intervenient psalmody, gospel acclamation, preaching, and the cantatas and concertatos this progression has stimulated. The chorale has been the musical center. The chorale and its related music have nourished and formed Lutherans and led them to a large and remarkable repertoire generation after generation. Lutherans, among them Paul Manz, have contributed this to their brothers and sisters in other confessional groups, just as other groups have contributed their resources to Lutherans.

What needs to be noted here is that neither Lutherans nor the whole church and world are served by avoiding or forgetting the goodly Lutheran heritage, just as other groups do not serve themselves or others well by avoiding or forgetting theirs. Paul Manz did not forget. Communities do not develop and do good in the world as generalized mush. They have a specificity that relates to the specificity of the incarnation and their vocation. The Lutheran chorale heritage, what it stimulated and still stimulates, and what Paul Manz contributed to it, are significant, specific, and formative contributions to the whole church catholic, to be prized among us for our good and for the good of our neighbors.

V. Style

Let's suppose that you knew nothing about Paul Manz. You skimmed Scott Hyslop's book about Manz, *The Journey Was Chosen*, including the chapter there by David Cherwien, which is titled "Symbolism," but is about much more. Or you glanced at James Freese's biography of Manz with Cherwien's foreword and its parentheses on the first page about the combination of a 32' reed with a 1' flute.[12] You would know immediately that

---

12. Freese, *Paul O. Manz: The Enduring Legacy of the Hymn Festival*, 5.

the goodly heritage and its particular Lutheran insights did not only live in the realm of theoretical thought for Manz. They took musical shape. That shape, however, was not a legalistic repristination of some sort, nor was it some new, idiosyncratic, presumably brilliant invention which our age likes to champion as "outside the box." It learned from and used the formal and syntactical musical structures derived from the church's heritage through its Lutheran insights, lived into and with ears attuned to our time and place. Or, in Cherwien's words, Manz's hymn festivals "were an interesting juxtaposition of the known with the unexpected."[13]

Because we avoid the joined wisdom of theological and musical insights, once technique is taken for granted, we gravitate to questions of musical style determined by whatever we think will further our own particular interests. When this becomes, as in our period, what has been called "missional," it reveals yet another version of works' righteousness where we, by our works, think we can get people into God's presence. So our worship wars in recent years have been characterized by assaults on one another to further our own private opinions, after which we retreat behind stylistic barricades.

Styles are important. I have tried to detail some of these and their attendant issues in *Church Musicians: Reflections on Their Call, Craft, History, and Challenges*.[14] I do not want to downplay their importance. But to reduce our conversations or lack thereof to matters of style is to avoid central issues. It leads us not only to a generalized mistake, but to idealizing certain practitioners on one or another side of these battles in our cultural star-studded system.

With someone like Paul Manz, that means we are tempted to take precisely what he did as the way all church musicians should do everything. He would probably be the first to warn us against this sort of idolatry. I have heard informed discussions of able church musicians where there were disagreements about any number of issues, like a tempo Manz took, or the space he left between stanzas of a hymn, or running around the circle of fifths. Every time I heard one of these conversations, I thought that if Manz himself had been present he would have joined the discussion with a point of view that took into account what was being said without dismissing it, though he would have had and would have expressed opinions about it— kindly. He was kind enough to encourage even organists like me, and to see that we had something to contribute. The conversations I had with him

---

13. Freese, 5.
14. Westermeyer, *Church Musicians*, 59–71.

about church music were generally beyond any specific organ playing, and they were always thoughtful, gentle, and characterized by a reluctance to criticize harshly even if he had been treated badly, though he had definite and carefully thought-out opinions.

We will not be well served by regarding Paul Manz or J. S. Bach or any human being, no matter how able, as exemplifying the only way to do something. Manz and Bach teach us all sorts of things that include styles and techniques along with the craft that is required of church musicians. But they also teach us that we are to employ our particular competencies and skills in the contexts of and with the people we serve. They both wrote occasional music for the occasions, people, and places in which they worked. Judgments about style and what does and does not fit are not only local ones, of course. These come from across the church's history with its wisdom, as Bach and Manz both teach us. They also teach us that we are not in their circumstances, as they are not in ours. As they in their circumstances did what they were called to do, so we in ours have the same call to music in the service of the gospel. Let us each figure it out in the places where we work, in connection with the help of our past and present colleagues—Paul Manz among them. And, like Paul Manz, let us do this with all of its duty and delight.

20

Justice and Peace

For the March 2017 issue of *Pipenotes*, I cited the Hymn Festival at Sinai Lutheran Church in Fremont, Nebraska, referenced in Chapter 17, then added the next three paragraphs.

The hymn festival at Sinai Church symbolized a remarkable breadth. It celebrated the 125th anniversary of a particular church in a particular place in a particular tradition, including the 500th anniversary of the Reformation; but it did this as part of the song of the whole church catholic. All of the other hymn festivals I knew about during 2017 did the same thing. Reformation anniversaries have been tempted to celebrate hatred between those who could not talk to one another, but Reformation hymn festivals in 2017 have emphasized the constructive, life-giving role that organs and church musicians play in spite of the circumstances they face.

This is striking. In a time when the world is cracking apart with hatred and greed, organs in worship services and hymn festivals are helping people sing together, people who may not be able to talk to each other. In addition, we are all gifted with sounds that are deeply related to our particular time and place, but equally related to many times and places in many languages and styles. This provides a welcome embrace for all of us who may or may not share points of view, and for all of us in and beyond ourselves as we hear ever old and new worlds of sound, with ever old and new worlds of insights.

This is also subversively constructive—and joyful. Do not believe the culture's words of sadness and death, filtered through our hatred and greed. As Martin Luther King, Jr., said, the arc of history tends toward justice and peace, appearances notwithstanding. As Barack Obama has said, that arc does not proceed by itself. We have to grasp and bend it. The organ and those who play it are part of that arc and its bending. Ride out the arc. Follow the wisdom of Pope Francis: joyfully sing—and play—as you go.

+ + +

The larger picture into which the preceding comments fit, a central subtheme of this book, is that doxology drives justice and peace.[1] The Psalms, Mary's Song (the Magnificat in Luke 1:46–53 which is the central song of the church), the Ordinary of the Mass, the Propers of the Mass, and the biblical readings all lead the church to work for justice and peace. Much of this, sometimes all of it, has been sung. It is the literature with which church musicians work, day in and day out. So, along with the whole church but in an especially intense way, church musicians and poets invariably are led to concerns for justice and peace.

None of the following therefore is accidental:[2]

- The Psalms invariably lead from doxology to justice, as in Psalm 33, which begins by rejoicing in the Lord, and a few verses later notes that God loves righteousness and justice.

- Miriam's congregational song in Exodus 15:21 and Moses' longer solo song in Exodus 15:1–18 are about the deliverance of the people from oppression and bondage.

- The Last Words of David, the person most associated with the Psalms, in 2 Samuel 23:1–7, are about ruling justly.

- Hannah's song in 1 Samuel 2:1–10 and Mary's song which echoes it are about raising up the lowly.

- The peace—the peace God bestows in Christ—at the beginning of the Mass sung in the Gloria is shared at the kiss of peace during the Mass, and is sung again in the Agnus Dei at communion and leads to the church's going into the world in peace to serve the Lord.

- Paul in Colossians 3:16 commended the church's singing for the glory of God and the good of the neighbor.

---

1. Westermeyer, *Let Justice Sing: Hymnody and Justice.*

2. For a similar list, see Chapter 17.

- At the time of the Barmen Declaration[3] against the Nazis in Germany, a prophetic neo-Baroque or neo-Renaissance soundscape was employed among musicians like Hugo Distler, Ernst Pepping, and Helmut Walcha.[4]

- Olivier Messiaen wrote his *Quartet for the End of Time* in a Nazi prison camp, and challenged the status quo in the rest of his music with a soundscape organically related to the church's concern for grace and peace that counters the world's agenda.

- David Cherwien and the National Lutheran Choir sang a prophetic program titled *The Caged Bird Sings.*

Church musicians are not usually visible leaders of crusades or causes for justice, peace, and a social order in which the neighbor and the common good are prized; but they and the music they lead are far more important and significant in this regard than may at first seem apparent. Under the surface, like a single mustard seed, church music and its musicians signify and embody God's gift—a subversively constructive and life-giving gift—to our fallen world in the song of the creation and the new creation. This is sometimes necessarily couched in confrontational language, but more often it comes even more powerfully and just as necessarily with the doxological, parabolic, liturgical, and poetic cast that Emily Dickinson described so well.

> Tell all the Truth but tell it slant —
> Success in Circuit lies
> Too bright for our infirm Delight
> The Truth's superb surprise
>
> As Lightning to the Children eased
> With explanation kind
> The Truth must dazzle gradually
> Or every man be blind —[5]

---

3. The Barmen Declaration was adopted in 1934 in the city of Barmen, Germany, by confessing Christians. They objected to the Nazi ideology and to making the church subservient to the state.

4. These were church musicians, teachers, and composers whose work and music undercut what was acceptable to and desired by the Nazis. Distler, the organist at the St. Jacobi Church in Lübeck where he restored his predecessor Buxtehude's Vesper series, was Jan Bender's teacher. Bender took the tune Distler was commissioned to compose for the takeover of Austria and let out its essence with Martin Franzmann's text "Weary of All Trumpeting." Pepping taught at the Spandau School of Church Music and composed a three-volume organ book with music for the whole church year. Walcha was a blind organist at the Friedenskirche in Frankfurt am Main who wrote chorale preludes for organ and twice recorded the complete works of Bach.

5. Johnson, ed. *The Complete Poems of Emily Dickinson*, 506, #1129.

The truth comes veiled in flesh, hidden in a manger and in the vocations of carpenters and musicians—lived out unseen for the least of these, spoken in parables, stretched out under the suffering of a cross, and sung on the slant so that we all, in all of our infirmity and weakness, may be able to behold it and be filled with its brightness.

21

The Church and Its Musicians, Including Organists

Attacks

Organs and organists are especially under attack in our period, as I indicated in Chapters 6 and 8. This is partly, as I have said, because of the systemic divide in the American church between the study of music and the study of theology, partly because of cultural shifts and changes that tend to undercut the arts generally, partly because of the suspicion about anybody who has authority, which includes those who have studied and practiced a musical art that is not a popular one, partly because of the cultural tendency to view music as a sales tool, and partly because of the inclination of our time to pay little, if any, attention to wisdom we may glean from our sisters and brothers who came before us. The organ's long history, in times and places that are not ours, make it especially vulnerable because it challenges us by transcending, crossing, and countering our cultural framework. (See below under **Culture** for more about this.) There are those who want to abandon it. Some responses need to be made to this point of view. The basic question before us is whether or not we need organs for the music of the church in its worship.

Voices and Instruments

The answer to that question is no, organs are not strictly necessary for worship. We don't have to have any instruments at all. We only need human beings and their voices, as in the early church and in the Eastern Orthodox church which has followed this practice. To say we don't have to have organs, however, does not help us very much and begs subsequent questions. Do we need buildings, books, baptismal fonts, altars, pulpits, or icons? No. We could do what we need to do at worship with people singing and speaking biblical and liturgical words around water, bread, and wine in a clearing in the woods, or in a parking lot, or under a shelter somewhere. But, given what the church has bequeathed to us in the physical and visual environments it has created, and how these environments have helped people pray and proclaim the gospel, are we wise to junk them?

As to the organ, the early church found its associations, like those of other musical instruments at the time, to be idolatrous and immoral.[1] For the last millennium, however, the church in the West has found the pipe organ to be shorn of those associations and to have the least idolatrous and immoral associations of any instrument. A huge repertoire has been developed for it, more related and better suited to the church's song than any other instrument. That repertoire is both congregational and choral. The organ, more than any other instrument, points to the happy symbiosis where neither the congregational nor the choral part gets to dominate or obscure the other.

The organ has helped people pray and proclaim the gospel in alternation and conjunction with the church's singing. It makes sounds with breath through pipes just like the human voice, and it has one sound for each pipe so that pipes together are needed to form a community, just like people singing together. Invariably, it is at least slightly out of tune, which yields a communal effect also just like human voices singing together. Not only has it been and continues to be closely related to the church's song, both for the music of the assembly and of the choir, but it also has made and continues to make valuable contributions to the church and the culture as a solo instrument and in ensembles with voices and other instruments. Furthermore, it points to God's gift of music with or without words, an insight Luther gives us,[2] and it points to a city of love that works together, as I indicated in Chapter 12. And then there is the organ's sheer delight. For that—along with serious and humorous historical, cultural, communal, and musical comments—see Haig Mardirosian's collected columns in his book *Vox Humana*.

Iconoclasm

Attacks on the organ are one form of iconoclasm in our age. If the task of the church is to destroy whatever it inherits and continually to start from scratch generation after generation, then organs and virtually anything

---

1. See Stappert, *A New Song for an Old World: Musical Thought in the Early Church.*

2. Anttila, *Luther's Theology of Music,* 84–97.

and everything else that is part of our crafting of the created order can be destroyed and forgotten. The church catholic, however, has continually assumed that it can and should not only craft the created order as well as possible, but that it should learn from those who crafted it before us.[3] Iconoclastic movements have generally resulted in regret and in attempts to reverse them. I share the church catholic's assumption and recommend it to our next generation. We are best served by learning what we can from the organ past and present, using it well, and building on what it has taught us.

The Organ and Other Instruments

To use the organ well does not imply using only the organ. Other instruments are welcome to the party, at least in the West, as is common among organists who employ a wide palette of musical styles, voices, and instruments in their planning, playing, and conducting. The problem here is not using other instruments, but excluding the organ. As a general rule, that is a bad idea, as some churches which omitted it in their building projects found later, when they regretted that decision.

Poor Use of Instruments

Using the organ well also implies that it can be used poorly, which is very true. Its poor use has sometimes been given as the reason for junking it. The curious thing about that reason is that the replacements for the organ tend to replicate its poor use. For example, the organ has been criticized for being too loud and drowning out the people's voices. Instruments and voices with microphones have been substituted to rectify the problem, but they make the same mistake in spades. I have been told repeatedly about churches where amplified groups are said to be leading hearty congregational singing. When I visit, I find that the singers and players making loud sounds through microphones are all that can be heard. No one else is singing, with the exception of a few people who, though drowned out, may mouth words now and then. That is hardly hearty congregational singing. Better singing invariably seems to be present where there are organs, even if they are used poorly. That does not justify the poor use of organs, but points instead to a curious contradiction that does not solve the problem and may well intensify it.

---

3. Luther is among those who cogently summarize this. See Chapters 16 and 17.

Culture

Accompanying this contradiction is what may be a well-intentioned presupposition which I have heard from some of the folks who use microphones. "Since people in our culture do not sing," they say, "we will sing for them." That, however, solves little and again compounds the problem. The human race longs to sing, even though our culture discourages and quashes that longing. The church is not well served by collapsing into the culture. As the Nairobi Statement says, the church is not only contextual, transcultural, and cross-cultural. It is also counter-cultural.[4] The organ brings with it all four of those components, including the counter-cultural one. It may be a prime symbol that tells us truth is not a product to be sold with music as its marketing tool. We are well advised to heed its wisdom, sing as we go, and help others sing. The organ is our ally on the pilgrim journey.

Stewardship

The organ is not only our ally in its association with these four cultural components, it is also our ally in stewardship. We are called to steward our resources well, to make our meeting places of the highest possible quality for the glory of God, but then to look outward beyond them on behalf of the poor and needy.[5] That means spending wisely, not gaudily or foolishly, on our gatherings at worship where God graces us and sends us out. Pipe organs, among them mechanical action ones, are stewardly expenditures. Over the long haul, they are less expensive than continual replacements. They provide high quality and last for generations with the four components of the Nairobi Statement.

Investing in church organists—that is, church organists with musical and theological study, not people who happen to play the organ in church—is also a stewardly move. Organists should be paid well like everybody else, but they cost less than groups of musicians. They can coordinate things much more efficiently than a group can, with both pastors and the rest of the church, and they provide a wider stylistic grid of healthy musical juxtapositions than most other musicians or groups are able to give in the same circumstances.

Cost is not the fundamental issue, however. Church musicians, including organists—because they deal with psalms, hymns, spiritual songs, and the repertoires these have spawned in worshiping contexts that

---

4. The Lutheran World Federation, "Nairobi Statement on Worship and Culture."

5. See Tornielli and Galeazzi, *This Economy Kills: Pope Francis on Capitalism and Social Justice*, 4ff.

span past centuries and the present—often, if not usually, know more about the church's worship than pastors do, because pastors' programs of theological study generally lack worship and music. Church musicians cannot avoid such study even though they have been systemically shut out of the official theological dialogue, and some fine programs where they have been included have been shut down. Church musicians learn what they need to learn by seeking it out against the odds. They have something important to contribute to our common life which is more than technical facility.

Talk to Them

For years, I have received reports from musicians who have been abused by their pastors, either subtly or not so subtly. Pastors who do this are not bad people. They have simply been trained in a system which says they have the requisite education, and musicians do not and are artist/technicians with little or nothing to contribute to the common life of the church beyond musical skills. Different skill sets and backgrounds are regarded as temperamental problems. Musicians are as sinful as pastors and controlled by the same bifurcated system, but the power differential between the two makes the abuse of musicians more normative than the abuse of pastors. Some musicians therefore have told me that they wanted to go to seminary to be ordained in order to gain as much power as the clergy.

Power is not a reason for ordination. Preaching the Word and presiding at font and table are the reasons for ordination. Forty years ago, Erik Routley addressed the matter of ordaining church musicians. Here is what he said:

> A musician is an artist employed by the church who hopes to be able to give what he or she has for the edifying of God's people. To lay hands on the musician in ordination would be not only anomalous; it would probably become an excuse for doing no more. No, don't lay hands on the musicians. Talk to them.[6]

When I wrote the article that is now Chapter 14 in this book, I sent it to Paul Landahl, whom I reference there. He had since become the bishop of the Evangelical Lutheran Church in Chicago and then served the Lutheran School of Theology at Chicago. I asked if what I had written was OK with him. He not only said yes with thanks, but added that when he encounters complaints from pastors about their musicians, he says to the pastors, "Talk to them."

---

6. Routley, *Church Music and the Christian Faith*, 138.

The advice of Routley and Landahl is well taken. We are wise to follow it. We are justified by grace through faith. We are made free to disagree with one another and figure things out together for the common good, even when our systems divide us. We can talk honestly and figure things out.

We are not justified by our works of agreement or disagreement, nor are we justified by our works that we falsely think will keep the church in business. We can trust that God in Christ through the Holy Spirit will sustain the church. We don't have to worry about that and have nothing to fear. We are made free. God "sends us forth…into our world of pain to do what we [are] meant to do in Jesus' name,"[7] with the checks and balances of our community in our particular time and place.

The church is often defined in the popular mind as exactly what it is not called to be: legalistic, closed in on itself, and characterized by hurtful human works. We should not be surprised these impressions are part of what drive people like the "nones" and "dones" away from the church. We may have helped to foster them. The church may have internal battles which compound the problem, and for which we also bear some responsibility. We can and are called to confess our sins—repeatedly—and to do our work on the path of God's grace.

Our institutions may collapse and die. The church has witnessed the collapse of institutions and empires before. That is not our worry. The message with which we are entrusted transcends the culture, its mistakes, its misunderstandings, and our contributions to them. What phoenix will emerge from the ashes of our time is not known, nor ours to worry about. It will not be evident until after most of us are dead, though there are witnesses to what might be on the horizon—as in the past. For example, we know that the church is made up of sinners who are nonetheless some of the most remarkable and caring people in the world. We know that the church engages in some of the most caring and responsible work for others, especially those in need. We know that the church makes some of the finest music and that it includes organs and organ-building. We know that there are schools which have not betrayed the church and which support vigorous church music programs, as do some local churches and newly-arising groups like the Church Music Institute in Dallas, Texas, or the Center for Church Music in River Forest, Illinois. In spite of all the rhetoric to the contrary, our problems are not what define us, nor do disagreements or

---

7. See the hymn by José Aguiar in the Preface.

generational divides or institutional collapses or money or numbers or momentary easy answers which soon evaporate.

The Holy Spirit can be trusted. The burden is easy, and the duty is delight. Get to work. Talk to one another, and include church musicians—among them the organists—in the conversations. They will likely bring to the table the insight of Paul in Colossians 3:16, and what the church and its musicians have learned again and again throughout the church's history: that church music is for the glory of God and the good of the neighbor. Though contextual, it is not a sales technique in the culture's normal view. Precisely what that means is what we each are called to figure out in connection with the wisdom of the whole church past and present.

If you are new to the journey, welcome. If you are already traveling along the road, continue to savor its delight. That delight includes the sounds of Truth. They are not the sounds of our culture's superficial glitz, but ones which, as Emily Dickinson put it, "dazzle gradually."

Acknowledgments

Though this is a small book, a large number of people have contributed to it and need to be thanked, starting with my wife Sally for making it possible for me to do this work. I am grateful to the members of the Twin Cities Chapter of the American Guild of Organists and its Board, to whom this book is dedicated, for the privilege of working with them on things that matter in their constructively collegial spirit. For specific chapters, I thank Robin Knowles Wallace, Editor of *The Hymn,* who requested the articles that became the second section of this book; Paul Landahl whom I reference in Chapter 14; Hilary Donaldson and the Program Committee of the 2017 Hymn Society Conference for the invitation to give a plenary address that became Chapter 17; Robert A. Hausman, David Jenkins, Kristin Rongstad, John S. Setterlund, Don Luther, and the Worship Dialogue for help with Chapter 18; David Cherwien for asking me to address the 2016 Manz Tage conference at Mount Olive Lutheran Church in Minneapolis, published in *CrossAccent* and appearing here as Chapter 19; and Claire Bushong, David Schack, and Sinai Lutheran Church in Fremont, Nebraska, for the privilege of preparing the commentary for the 2017 hymn festival there with the Juget-Sinclair organ that stimulated the cover of this book and is referenced in Chapters 17 and 20. Thanks are also owed to the Lutheran Church of the Resurrection in Roseville, Minnesota—including Pastor Timothy Bernard, Interim Pastor Laura Thelander, and Cantor Gary Butler—for a healthy place to worship God and from which to live out care for the neighbor in our various vocations. For their contributions, thank you to Zebulon M. Highben, a former master of sacred music student at Luther Seminary, now the Director of the Concert Choir and Chamber Singers at Muskingum University, for the Foreword, and Neil Johnston, Chair of Fine and Performing Arts at Century College in White Bear Lake, Minnesota, and a fellow member at the Lutheran Church of the Resurrection, for the cover. And a final thank you to the publisher: Mark Lawson of MorningStar for collaborative and competent human contact rather than automated gridlock, for publishing books like this, and for suggesting the title; Caitlin Custer for her collegial, careful, and perceptive editing; and Kristen Schade for her cover, book design, and care for final details.

Bibliography

American Guild of Organists. *A Guide for Organ Committees.* 2016. DVD.

Anttila, Miikka E. *Luther's Theology of Music.* Berlin: Walter de Gruyter GmbH, 2013.

Association of Lutheran Church Musicians. "The Role of the Cantor." Poster.

Aufdemberge, C. T. *Christian Worship: Handbook.* Milwaukee: Northwestern Publishing House, 1997.

Bach, J. S. *Clavierübung, Dritter Theil: Choralvorspielen und Duetten.* Leipzig, 1739; New York: C. F. Peters, 1951.

Barone, Michael, prod. *Pipedreams.* American Public Media. St. Paul, MN.

Benbow, William. "The Function of Music in the Service of the Church." *The Lutheran Church Review* XVII (July 1898): 476–484.

Benson, Louis F. "Lecture One: The Apostolic Ideal of Hymnody." In *The Hymnody of the Christian Church: The Lectures on "The L. P. Stone Foundation" Princeton Theological Seminary.* Philadelphia: Westminster Press, 1927.

Bonhoeffer, Dietrich. *Life Together.* Translated by John W. Doberstein. New York: Harper & Brothers, 1954.

Boyd, Malcolm. *Bach.* Oxford: Oxford University Press, 2000.

Busted, Thomas D. "AGNUS DEI: The Cost of Discipleship." *The New Mercersburg Review* LVI (Spring 2017): 28–43.

Cherwien, Susan. "*Trutzlied* or *Trostlied*? A Hymnist Looks at Martin Luther's "Ein feste Burg," *Word and World* 34, no. 4 (October 2014): 387–397.

Clement, Albert. "A Case of Liturgical Practice in Johann Sebastian Bach's Home," in "Ars et Musica in Liturgia," *Essays Presented to Casper Honders on his Seventieth Birthday,* ed. Frans Brouwer and Robin Leaver. Metuchen: Scarecrow Press, 1994, pp. 32–55.

Committee for Ecumenical and Interreligious Affairs, United States Conference of Catholic Bishops, Evangelical Lutheran Church in America. *Declaration on the Way: Church, Ministry, and Eucharist.* Minneapolis: Augsburg Fortress, 2015.

Cox, Harvey. *The Market as God.* Cambridge: Harvard University Press, 2017.

David, Hans T. and Arthur Mendel. *The New Bach Reader: A Life of Johann Sebastian Bach in Letters and Documents.* New York: W. W. Norton, 1998.

Evangelical Lutheran Worship. Minneapolis: Augsburg Fortress, 2006.

Fisher, Alexander. *Music and Religious Identity in Counter-Reformation Augsburg, 1580–1630.* Vermont: Ashgate Publishing, 2004.

Fothergill, Chad. "Bach's Benediction: The E-flat Major Fugue, BWV 552, and the Christian Funeral Liturgy," *CrossAccent* 22, no. 3 (Fall/Winter 2014): 23–29.

———. "Doctor, Lawyer, Poet, Mayor…and Cantor? Early Lutheran Church Musicians and Vocation," *CrossAccent* 25, no. 1 (Spring 2017): 14–25.

Francis. *Laudate Si': On Care for Our Common Home* [Encyclical]. Rome: Vatican Press, May 24, 2015 (Pentecost).

Freese, James W. *Paul O. Manz: The Enduring Legacy of the Hymn Festival.* Minneapolis: Lutheran University Press, 2014.

Garcia-Rívera, Alejandro. *The Community of the Beautiful: A Theological Aesthetics.* Collegeville, MN: The Order of St. Benedict, Inc., 1999.

Gardiner, John Eliot. Bach: *Music in the Castle of Heaven.* New York: Alfred A. Knopf, 2013.

Geck, Martin. *Johann Sebastian Bach: Life and Work.* Translated by John Hargraves. Orlando: Houghton Mifflin Harcourt, 2006.

Guenther, Eileen. *Rivals or a Team? Clergy-Musician Relationships in the Twenty-First Century.* St. Louis: MorningStar Music Publishers, 2012.

Hefner, Philip. Review of *The Market as God,* by Harvey Cox. *The Christian Century* 134, no. 15 (July 2017): 41.

Heiges, Donald R. *The Christian's Calling.* Rev. ed. Philadelphia: Fortress Press, 1984.

Howard, Jay Norwood. "Johann Crüger as a Music Theorist: A Translation and Critical Commentary of his *Synopsis Musica* of 1630." MA Thesis, Ohio State University, 1968.

The Hymn Society in the United States and Canada. *Singing Welcome: Hymns and Songs of Hospitality to Refugees and Immigrants.* N. p.: n. p., 2017.

The Hymnal of the Evangelical and Reformed Church. St. Louis: Eden Publishing House, 1941.

Hymns Ancient and Modern for Use in the Service of the Church. London: Novello, 1861.

Hyslop, Scott M. *The Journey Was Chosen: The Life and Work of Paul Manz.* St. Louis, MorningStar Music Publishers, 2007.

Jenson, Robert W. *Systematic Theology, Volume 1: The Triune God.* Oxford: Oxford University Press, 1997.

Johnson, Thomas H., ed. *The Complete Poems of Emily Dickinson.* New York: Little, Brown and Company, 1961.

Keach, Benjamin. *The Breach Repair'd in God's Worship.* London, 1691.

Koriath, Kirby L. *Music for the Church: The Life and Work of Walter E. Buszin.* Fort Wayne, IN: The Good Shepherd Institute, 2003.

Krauth, Harriet Reynolds. *Church Book.* Philadelphia: General Council Publication Board, 1872.

Lathrop, Gordon. *Holy Things: A Liturgical Theology.* Minneapolis: Fortress Press, 1993.

Lawlor, Robert. "Geometry in the Service of Prayer: Reflections on Cistercian Mystic Architecture," *Parabola* 3, no. 1 (1981): 12–19

Lawrence, Joy. E and John A. Ferguson. *A Musician's Guide to Church Music.* New York: The Pilgrim Press, 1981.

Leaver, Robin. "Bach's 'Clavierübung III': Some Historical and Theological Considerations," *The Organ Yearbook* 6 (1975): 17–32.

Leo X. *Exsurge Domine* [Papal Bull]. Rome: 1520.

Luther, Martin. "A Preface for All Good Hymnals." 1538. Translated by Paul Nettl. In *Luther's Works,* Volume 53: Liturgy and Hymns. Edited by Ulrich S. Leopold. Philadelphia: Fortress Press, 1965.

———. "Preface to Georg Rhau's *Symphoniae iucundae*." 1538. Translated by Ulrich S. Leopold. In *Luther's Works*, Volume 53: Liturgy and Hymns. Edited by Ulrich S. Leopold. Philadelphia: Fortress Press, 1965.

———. *Luther's Works*, Volume 54: Table Talk. Translated and edited by Theodore G. Tappert. Philadelphia: Fortress Press, 1967.

Lutheran Service Book. St. Louis: Concordia Publishing House, 2006.

The Lutheran World Federation. "Nairobi Statement on Worship and Culture." In *Can We Talk*? Engaging in Worship and Culture. Evangelical Lutheran Church in America: 2016.

The Lutheran World Federation and The Pontifical Council for Promoting Christian Unity. *From Conflict to Communion: Lutheran-Catholic Commemoration of the Reformation in 2017*. Leipzig: Evangelische Verlagsanstalt GmbH, 2016.

Mardirosian, Haig. *Vox Humana*. St. Louis: MorningStar Music Publishers, 2017.

Marty, Martin E. "History-less Judgements," *Sightings* (August 8, 2016). https://divinity.uchicago.edu/sightings/history-less-judgments.

McKinnon, James. *The Temple, the Church Fathers, and Early Western Chant*. Aldershot: Ashgate, 1998.

Neale, John Mason. *Collected Hymns, Sequences, and Carols*. Edited by Mary Sackville Lawson. London: Hodder and Stoughton, 1914.

Page, Christopher. *The Christian West and Its Singers: The First Thousand Years*. New Haven: Yale University Press, 2010.

Paulsell, Stephanie. "When the market is God," *The Christian Century* 134, no. 12 (June 2017): 35.

Placher, William, ed. *Callings: Twenty Centuries of Christian Wisdom on Vocation*. Grand Rapids: William B. Eerdmans Publishing Company, 2005.

Ramshaw, Gail. *Words That Sing*. Chicago: Liturgy Training Publications, 1992.

Routley, Erik. *The Church and Music: An Enquiry into the History, the Nature, and the Scope of Christian Judgment on Music*. London: Gerald Duckworth & Co. Ltd, 1950.

———. *Church Music and the Christian Faith*. Carol Stream, IL: Agape, 1978.

———. *Church Music and Theology*. Philadelphia: Muhlenberg Press, 1959.

———. "Correspondence with an Anglican Who Dislikes Hymns," *The Presbyter* 6, no. 2 (Second Quarter 1948): 17.

Rowthorn, Jeffrey and Russell Schulz-Widmar, compilers and editors. *Sing of a World Made New: Hymns of Justice, Peace, and Christian Responsibility*. Carol Stream, IL: Hope Publishing Company, 2014.

Saliers, Don E. "Beauty, Holiness, and Everday," *The American Organist* 48, no. 6 (June 2014): 12.

Schweitzer, Albert. *J. S. Bach, Volume 1*. Translated by Ernest Newman. Boston: Bruce Humphries, 1911.

Stappert, Calvin R. *A New Song for an Old World: Musical Though in the Early Church*. Grand Rapids: William B. Eerdmans Publishing Company, 2007.

Tatlow, Ruth. *Bach's Numbers: Compositional Proportion and Significance*. Cambridge: Cambridge University Press, 2015.

Tertullian. *Treatise on the Resurrection*. Translated and edited by Ernest Evans. London: SPCK, 1969.

Tornielli, Andrea and Giacomo Galeazzi. *This Economy Kills: Pope Francis on Capitalism and Social Justice*. Translated by Demetrio S. Yocum. Collegeville, MN: Liturgical Press, 2015.

Trupp, Brian K. *A History of Trinity Lutheran Church*, 1751-2011. N. p., n. p., n. d.

Troeger, Thomas. *Wonder Reborn: Creating Sermons on Hymns, Music, and Poetry*. Oxford: Oxford University Press, 2010.

Westermeyer, Paul. *Church Musicians: Reflections on Their Call, Craft, History, and Challenges*. St. Louis: MorningStar Music Publishers, 2015.

———. *The Church Musician*. San Francisco: Harper & Row, 1988.

———. *The Church Musician: Revised Edition*. Minneapolis: Augsburg Fortress, 1997.

———. *Hymnal Companion to Evangelical Lutheran Worship*. Minneapolis: Augsburg Fortress, 2010.

———. "Hymn Performance: Perspective," *The Hymn* 68, no. 1 (Winter 2017): 40–41.

———. "Hymn Performance: Tempo," *The Hymn* 68, no. 2 (Spring 2017): 37–38.

———. "Hymn Performance: Breath," *The Hymn* 68, no. 3 (Summer 2017): 46–47.

———. "Hymn Performance: Texts and Music," *The Hymn* 68, no. 4 (Autumn 2017): 44–45.

———. "Johannes Riedel." *The Canterbury Dictionary of Hymnology*. Canterbury Press, http://www.hymnology.co.uk/j/johannes-riedel.

———. "Music and the Reformation: An Ecumenical Achievement." Plenary I at the Annual Conference of The Hymn Society, Waterloo, ON, July 2017.

———. *Let Justice Sing: Hymnody and Justice*. Collegeville, MN: Liturgical Press, 1998.

———. "Music and the Reformation: An Ecumenical Achievement." Plenary I at the Annual Conference of The Hymn Society, Waterloo, ON, July 2017, printed in *The Hymn* 68:4 (Autumn 2017): 7-12.

———. "Music in the Service of the Gospel: Discerning the Church Musician's Vocation through the Life and Work of Paul Manz," *CrossAccent* 25, no. 1 (Spring 2017): 5–13.

———. *Te Deum: The Church and Music*. Minneapolis: Fortress Press, 1998.

Williams, Peter. *Bach: A Musical Biography*. Cambridge: Cambridge University Press, 2016.

Wingren, Gustav. *Luther on Vocation*. Translated by Carl C. Rasmussen. Philadelphia: Muhlenberg Press, 1957.

Witvliet, John D. "Commemorating the Reformation for the 500th Time." *Reformed Worship* (blog). June 6, 2016. https://www.reformedworship.org/blog/commemorating-reformation-500th-time.

Wolff, Christoph. *Johann Sebastian Bach: The Learned Musician*. New York: W. W. Norton, 2000.

Index